2017 BOOK OF SCREEDS

JIM ACKERMAN

CONTENTS

JANUARY

Diminution of the Democratic Party

Those of us on the left are bemoaning the diminution of the Democratic Party. The truth is that the disfranchisement of the current Party has roots fifty years in the past, making the solution a hard row to hoe because policy is not the cure. Anybody can think up good policy. Generating allegiance requires showing care. Conversely, its polar opposite, indifference, can be long-lived.

In 1964, the Mississippi Freedom Democratic Party was turned away from the Presidential Convention at Atlantic City, after the standard Mississippi Democratic Party members had abandoned it. When the Freedom Party was later offered a compromise, two things happened. One, the convention result disenchanted the vast body of young white organizers, who walked away. Two, the compromise accepted the black professionals, doctors, lawyers, and the like, but turned away the working poor, the sharecroppers, and the domestic servants of the original coalition. In other words, the common people were refused their seats.

Even though the effect on Lyndon Johnson was to push through the Voting Rights Act and achieve the central goal of the SNCC, CORE, and the NAACP, a substantial number of the disaffected Mississippi Democrats never recovered their enthusiasm for the vote. It was diverted in two main streams, a hard turn left and a lingering deep cynicism about the political process as a social form.

These people, their philosophical progeny, and onlookers who were dispirited by their example are still outside the main stream. Somehow the wary and the cynical must be brought back into the fold if the Democratic Party is to stand up to the hegemony of the minority Republican Party and force compromises on it.

It will not be easy because the Republicans are fighting for a mythical tradition. Since it never actually existed in the complete form that they have confabulated, they can simply make it up as they go along, and this is the kitchen where they cook. You never beat people in their own kitchen. They know where all the utensils are.

Propaganda Style: Trump and Goebbels

Some recent comparisons between the disinformation mannerisms of the Trump horde and the propaganda machine of Joseph Goebbels, while seeming a little stretched, are neither inept nor out of place. One can easily take it too far, however, and the danger is not in misreading the present. It lies in misreading the Nazi past.

When it comes to propaganda, the current practitioners are rank amateurs. If you keep to the strategy of lies, half-lies, and damn lies, and the occasional vague threat of reprisal, the Trump team is adept enough, as long as a slap in the face now and then is okay. For Goebbels, the dissimulation was only part of the campaign. The rest was theater on a grand scale. Rallies were held on a giant venue outdoors, against monumental backdrops, at night when people are tired and suggestible, in a brightly-lighted setting with deep darkness all around. Deafening loudspeakers played energetic home-grown martial music during entrance and exit.

By a bewildering contrast, the theme music we hear from Trump is the Rolling Stones, the most enigmatic and nihilistic of the early British teen-idol bands. "Paint it, paint it, paint it. Paint it black."

The Nazi argumentation, although somewhat similar to the current inferences, starting with dire warnings and ending with hope, is more convincing to a homogeneous people like the Germans, who had been ruined by measures imposed on them by foreign powers, than to a divided country like America today.

The success of the German propaganda was conditioned by a decade of violence, intimidation, and thuggery by Nazi operators. The country had been the intermittent scene of civil war in the industrial regions and the southern border areas for nearly a decade. Equally unsettling were the internal controls. The SA, a mob of perverted psychopaths, the SS, a cadre of stiff-necks obsessed with record-keeping, the Gestapo, a paramilitary police force, and various troupes of loosely-organized amateur thugs motivated by nationalism, alcohol, and bloodlust were relentless in their demands for uniformity of opinion. Informers turned in their friends and neighbors. Children were recruited to the militarism. State agents attended the church sermons to take notes on legal compliance by the clergy.

Media control was absolute. From state-mandated radio programming, the blaring of propaganda and martial music through public loudspeakers, to the effective movies of Leni Riefenstahl, the propaganda campaign was expert and comprehensive. Unlike the Trumpist carnival game of now-you-see-it, now-you-don't, the mass state was a case study of mass psychological conditioning. It took more than a few well-placed transparent lies to get it across.

Vicente <u>Fox</u> <u>on</u> <u>Trump</u> <u>and</u> <u>Hitler</u>

Earlier today, former Mexican President Vicente Fox was excoriated on MSNBC for comparing Donald Trump to Adolf Hitler. Of course, Fox had overstated the case and, when pressed to explain himself, he stumbled in making the comparison believable.

Nevertheless, he had had a point. There are several similarities. Both Trump and Hitler are self-absorbed, narcissistic, defensive, displaying the classic overcompensating tendencies of the inferiority complex. Neither of them have any compunctions about expressing himself, although the presentation is often loose and rambling and the logic lacking. Stimulated by the belief that their country is the greatest ever and that it is driven by a people unsurpassed in morality and aptitude, they are both economic protectionists.

This last is where the similarities start to dissolve. Hitler was so protectionist that his aim was to create a German autarky, i.e., a completely self-contained economy that needed no international trade whatever. Obviously this is utter nonsense, since Germany did not have the goods for it, until Hitler's unique foreign policy is taken into account: "Wherever there are Germans, there is Germany." There are Germans everywhere, so everywhere is

Germany. The inference is clearly that Germany must take over the world. World domination is the aim.

With Trump, personal fortune and global sales of goods made in America are the aims. This is a strange and superfluous aim, inasmuch as Trump is already wealthy and the United States is the world's leader in so many ways that it is hard to count them, and it has been since the end of World War II. It is true, yes, that in some ways this is not so clear now as then. In 1950 the American economy represented 54% of the global GDP. Now it is about 18%, but this is not because America slipped. It is that the rest of the world caught up.

And this leads to the last similarity. Both men want to restore a greatness that once existed. In Hitler's case, German greatness had been short-lived and ruined by ill-advised warfare. America, however, was already and still is a great nation. The problem is not that it has been overtaken. It is not broken down on the finish line. If anything, it needs a tune-up, not a rebuild. And this is where all similarities end.

<u>Fact-checking</u> and <u>Truth-telling</u>

When it comes to the Trump Administration, fact-checking and truth-telling will always take second place, or further down the list of research, because it is behaving like an advertising agency. When you want to sell hand soap, you simply say it is the best and you praise it in the highest terms. It has this in it, it has that in it, you will love it, it will make you feel great. It is not necessary to convince people that they want soap. They already know this.

You say it has extraordinary powers coming from the ingredients whether it is true or not. It will clean because it is soap, and all soap is basically the same chemically. No soap is really good for your skin. By definition, soap degrades skin slightly. This truth does not stop people from buying soap. Therefore, most soaps contain oils and emollients that purport to repair the damage and make your skin better.

Okay, the facts aside, you prepare the mythology. You call your soap American Supremacy, and you bill it as the best soap to clean off the dirt of terrorism. Your slogan is, The Soap that will Make America Clean Again. Of course, the Americans already have soap. They know about soap, so they have to be convinced that this soap will clean better. If this fails, people have to be shamed into buying it. If you don't buy American Supremacy soap, you will still have dirt on your skin. Although it will not be true, a percentage of people will believe it because you say things like, "See these terrorists? They are dirty because they don't use American Supremacy soap." And you see a picture of a dirty person. A portion of the public will believe almost anything, and you can prove this to yourself by listening to people waiting in the grocery line, or the bank teller line, or the fast food line.

The next step is to tell people that they will *feel* dirty if they don't buy and use American Supremacy soap exclusively. Here's where the advertising campaign bogs down. Advertising, like politics, is the art of addition. You want to increase your market interest. You want to make people feel good for joining in, not to feel bad for staying away. This was demonstrated by the disastrous Schlitz beer "gusto" campaign in the mid-seventies. Young beer drinkers nowadays will be shocked to learn that Schlitz was then the number two beer in the country. Then came the massive "go for the gusto" campaign that featured an angry spokesman saying things like, "Don't you dare take away my gusto!" Schlitz went into a tailspin, regardless of quality, and the brand nearly disappeared.

You don't need to sell the Trump brand to the 46% of people who already buy it. If you can't get the sales figure over 50%, however, eventually you will lose the sales battle. Your opponents will be doing everything they can to sell their own soap.

<u>Trade</u> <u>Policy</u> <u>Differences</u>

When all the differences between the White House and the traditional Republicans in Congress are boiled out of the trade policy mix, the gook left over looks like a strong-dollar policy. Whether it is called "border adjustment" or an "import tariff" or an equalization of import fees and corporate taxes, the end result in monetary terms will be the depreciation of foreign currencies against the dollar.

While the intended effect of the tax and tariff policies is to increase exports while decreasing imports, the strong dollar trend will have the opposite effect. If foreign currencies depreciate by more than twenty per cent, on balance more will be imported than exported. In addition, the strong dollar will discourage tourism to the United States and encourage foreign tourism by Americans, further damaging the balance of trade.

We went through this in the nineteen eighties. By mid-decade, not only were consumer exports weak on account of the dollar's appreciation. Domestic steel and capital-goods production had degraded so far that the rest of the world was forced to turn to other countries for steel fabrication and factory design and manufacture. American large capital goods sales were nearly nonexistent. The balance-of-trade equation was so weighted against the dollar that the German and Japanese investors who held the biggest lots of American bonds were threatening a sell-off. It was becoming dis-economic to hold American paper.

The only thing that prevented the dollar from going into free-fall in 1986 was James Baker dunning the nations of the Group of Seven into accepting trade-weighted devaluations of the dollar by an aggregate 45% or so. The foreign investors in American paper would take a bath, but they reasoned that half of something was better than all of nothing. If this happened today, it is hard to believe that any diplomatic figure on the American scene could hope to accomplish any comparable remedy. Certainly, no one in the current White House has the strength, dash, and intelligence to get it done.

<u>Opinion</u> <u>Polls</u> <u>on</u> <u>Fraudulent</u> <u>Voting</u>

Opinion polls do not analyze random samples. They analyze "randomized" samples. They are not arbitrary. Therefore the first thing that has to be done is prepare the appropriate samples. This can be done in various ways, and qualifying questions are developed to produce a randomized sample. By the same token, the sample can be manipulated.

One of the common ways to produce a sample weighted one way or the other is by clever use of double negatives, sometimes combined with verbs such as "deny" or "affirm." For example, this question could be asked: "Could you affirm that you are not a non-citizen?" This could be answered, "Yes, I am not a non-citizen." It could also be answered, "No, I am not a non-citizen."

If you want a "randomized" sample of people in which a certain percentage of people will answer "yes" to the question, "did you vote?", even if none of the respondents actually voted and were non-citizens, it can be predicted by clever polling. All of this is made easier by dealing with people who speak English as a second language and who speak Spanish first, where the double negative has different usage rules. Thus the polling of resident alien populations in the United States can be made into a fraudulent exercise in false findings.

In any case, all the respondents from Honduras, Guatemala, El Salvador, and Nicaragua have experience in their home nations where the government itself rigs the ballot, where individual voter fraud can be a *de facto* death sentence and the secret ballot is a convenient fiction. Undocumented Central American immigrants are so unlikely to participate in voter fraud by the millions because of their home traditions that it would be hilarious to fake the statistics if it were not so preposterous. So, you manipulate the polling questions instead and present polling numbers that seem real but are simply made up.

FEBRUARY..

Where Have All the Racists Gone?

We know there is not the remotest possibility that all the followers of Donald Trump are misogynists, race-baiters, xenophobes, white supremacists, and autocraphiles. By the same token, we must also realize that all the racists, male chauvinists, immigrant-haters, and white nationalists who cast ballots did so in favor of him. The remaining question then is how the decent people who voted for him could stand shoulder to shoulder with the mugs and why they have no compunction about staying silent on it.

It cannot be that the decent followers are ignorant of their rude bedfellows in the political game. The far right's cries for relief from their imaginary enemies are heard as well out in the sport utility vehicle suburbs as in the White House. It is hard to believe that the delusions of the worst of them are shared by the best. This would mean that all of them are clinically deluded. Since this barely seems possible, the decent people must be motivated either by fear or by the kind of shame that provokes silence on the subject, that the silence might make the warped minds disappear as if by magic.

Obviously the leaders of the Trump movement are not afraid or ashamed, because they know that otherwise, their margin of electoral victory could not have been reached. They knew that all those ballots cast from the far right fringe could not go anywhere but to them, and so the possible conclusions are obvious: Either 1) the leaders openly welcome the fringe elements to the tent or 2) they are using the fringe cynically to pack the ballot boxes. Whether it is the one or the other, the peril is the same. The fringe may eventually be whipped up into a frenzy if their demands for supremacy are not met.

If this eventuates, tamping it down will not be easy, especially if the people in charge accommodate the sentiment. They have already started down this path by acting to remove the white supremacists and their kin from the list of national security threats. We can hardly expect vigilance to come from them. We could hope, at least, that the plain-vanilla conservatives would stand up and be counted, and we could hope that they have at least the semblance of a backbone to do so. Otherwise we and the world are in for a rough time of it for a while.

<u>Donald Trump and Bill O'Reilly</u>

When Donald Trump looked Bill O'Reilly in the eye and asked the rhetorical question, "You think Americans are so innocent?", every American who saw the tape sat up and said, "What?" They all saw something hinky in it. It offended the exceptionalists on the false equivalence, and it offended America's critics too, when they perceived the complete lack of contrition by Trump for American excesses.

On the facts of the issue concerning foreign policy, the United States has done plenty of meddling overseas, with mixed effect, and at times the federal government has acted like a predatory business agent for overseas sales. It can be argued both ways whether all this is bad or good, and every argument will find an intelligent sponsor. Even the most hallowed of historical federal heroes, Abraham Lincoln, let loose an unintended consequence in his vision that the Union must stand, that the "more perfect union" clause in the Constitution predicated a state in perpetuity. Denying the right of self-determination to the Confederacy could hardly be held out as a *modus operandi* to oppressed foreign populations in their own countries.

All this can be argued over. On the other hand, it is unarguable that Trump was saying something altogether different. He was saying that it was okay for Putin not to be innocent because so many Americans have not been innocent. Even if this opinion is not the false equivalence that it looks like on its face, it cannot be right that one moral failing justifies another. The only reasonable presumption the Commander-in-Chief can make about the American government being peopled with killers is that it comes as an apology. Otherwise, American exceptionalism, besides being wrong-headed, is also a bad joke.

All governments resort to force. Abraham Lincoln did send federal troops to New York City during the conscription riots, and three hundred some citizens were killed, but what he did not do was burn the city down. By contrast, during the second phase of the Chechen separation, Vladimir Putin destroyed Grozny, flattening it to the ground with bombs and artillery fire. Two hundred thousand casualties. Lincoln jailed some newspapermen. Putin has had a couple dozen assassinated.

The idea that American perfidy, even on the unlikely chance that it could be demonstrated, exculpates Putin and Russia would be a real howler if it were not so ignorant. A President trying the sentiment on for size makes for nausea, and not the existential nausea of Jean-Paul Sartre, the doubt that anything really makes a difference. This made a difference. It made many sick to watch it. This is what America has come to. This low.

Politics as Warfare

Liberal-bashing has become the dinner table sport of the new conservative, as if it were one of the rules to get their meal ticket punched. You can't call yourself a good conservative unless you beat a liberal down with a stick: "Get over it! You lost the election!"

The conservatives are the ones who need to get over it. They won. They need to get on with it. The only reward you reap out of beating a dead horse is a tired arm.

Insofar as it invokes the notion of *caritas*, there is nothing wrong with liberalism. Live and let live is the byword, and the constitutional manifesto to promote the general welfare is the motto.

With every heartbeat, the new conservative invokes, not *caritas*, but *gravitas* as the touchstone of political worth. "We are serious people. We don't entertain silly unworkable idealism and then force everyone to agree. Scratch a liberal and you will find a tyrant underneath."

The trouble here is the self-defeating description. Either liberals are silly people without a brain in their collective head or they are unyielding self-important phonies who want to tell everybody else what to do and how to do it. Silliness is not how you get the hard nose it takes to get control of others and keep it.

The real enemy in the war over sociological correctness is objectification. Turning people into objects is the first article of every political opinion. People become the chattels of political perception. Therefore they only have personal worth in the degree that they will agree to join the club and follow the charter. Everybody else is only worth destroying.

This is where the seed of self-destruction is sown. When you make competition the aim of social life and destruction of the other the goal of disagreement, another enemy pops up with every gain. Then, instead of getting on with it, you spend all your time fighting battles. Being good at warfare is not the same as being good at the business of living.

<u>Gunslingers</u> <u>and</u> <u>Intellectuals</u>

For 48 years we have had a string of Presidents so different that it hardly seems likely the same polity could have elected them all. If you turn this history on its side and look through the portholes, however, the connection comes clear. Except for Gerald Ford, and only because he was appointed, they have all claimed to be change agents, some of them hope and change, and the others desperation and change, bookended by two political oddballs.

Richard Nixon was practically an oxymoron, an introvert addicted to politics. It was impossible to imagine him schmoozing a crowd, and in fact, what he mostly did instead was work on people by enlisting them in various shifting intrigues. Aside from his well-known crimes and not-so-well-known mob ties, he was the last really clever man in the White House, who railed against liberals while backing up so close to their social and economic policies that he nearly duplicated them as he faced the other direction. An intellectual who hated intellectuals, he was so paranoid he saw hatred everywhere he looked. As a consequence he himself evoked hatred and made the vision true. He invented the silent majority to get elected by contrasting them to Agnew's "nattering nabobs of negativism," the counter-culture.For the next several elections, we have the born-again Jimmy Carter to deliver us from the fallen,

Nixon's backwash, in order to install hope again. Then the former FDR devotee Ronald Reagan to change up from liberal indulgence and invigorate the belief in America while spouting fundamentally anti-American rhetoric about the evils of government. Then Bush, to change away from rhetoric and bring back confidence in government. Clinton came along to weave economic conservatism and liberal social policies together. The younger Bush, reformed cokehead and alcoholic and also born-again, to restore order to the conservative vision with a dose of compassion. And Obama with the frank hope and change campaign through the looking glass, hoping at first that hope would be enough.

Then along came Trump, the ultimate outsider. He came from outside politics altogether, and what he knew about it he had got from watching television. He had no loyalties. What he expected was loyalty to him. He was the lone gunslinger, leader of his own gang, dedicated to the dream of making the town safe. An expert on conspiracy theory, he held his own counsel on the world's dangers. Ignorant of everything else, he designed his own brand of paranoia, as Nixon had. It is no secret that of all recent Presidents, Nixon is the one he admires. And so we have come full circle from the silent majority to the forgotten American and devotion to the dark side of history, looking for desperation to inspire change. We have come a long way. In so doing we have gone nowhere too.

<u>Hippies</u> <u>and</u> <u>the</u> <u>New</u> <u>World</u>

Once again, as we did in 1972 and 1980 and 2000, we have to
suffer a referendum on the Sixties because of culture warriors in
the White House. This fight always attracts friends. Powerful
figures in Washington are still upset about the advent of the hippy
fifty years ago. They are loath to let a good whipping-boy go,
while the closest the new crew have come to a hippy are the
paisley kimonos and Mexican fringe vests in ageing relatives'
attics. Therefore their enemy is an effigy, the Demon Liberal.

The prevailing critique, as kooky as it is tedious, involves tarring
all Baby-boomers with the Me Generation brush, and lumping
them together as the Godless libertines of capitalism, leading in
turn to the boom-and-bust economies of the nineties and aught-
2000's, the collapse of shared values, and the "socialism" of the
Obama Presidency. Whether or not this analytic model has any
forensic value beyond a debate in a sociology class, it is vitiated by
history itself.

When leaders of the Vietnam war protests made the hard left turn,
convincing their own parents that they had gone bonkers heaped on
sedition, the culture war slipped out of their grasp. The 1976
election ushered in a watered-down social liberalism that diluted

the conflict, and then Reagan crushed it by his equally forceful anti-government message, diverting the counter-culture's fervor and rendering it harmless. The hippies started raising children, cut their hair, got jobs, and bought houses. A mortgage is a powerful incentive to conventionalize behavior.

This social transformation was ratified by the election of 1992, when the ex-hippy President Clinton married social liberalism to economic conservatism and became a Rockefeller Republican in everything but name. George W. Bush's intent was basically the same, cradling to his chest a Catholic Charities-style philosophy adjusted to fit his providential view of history, but events got in the way. Backlash against the ensuing economic disruption inspired the youth vote that kicked Obama over the top. The body politic, however, had been sliding *en bloc* to the right for so long that this center-right candidate was called a socialist, and still is.

Trump and his people intend to delete the whole lot and install a mythical shared-value society ripped out of Hollywood's B-flick version of the Fifties, sanitized boosterism in a society that applauded Eisenhower's brutal Operation Wetback. What they are missing about the Sixties, however, is something vital. The Greatest Generation taught its children well: believe in yourself, do what you think is right, and stick to your guns. The two generations disagreed on substance but when it came to sincerity they were like peas in a pod. The clash between sentiment and opinion was real, but there was still love in it. What we have now is hate alone.

<u>One-upmanship</u> <u>in</u> <u>the</u> <u>White</u> <u>House</u>

Many explanations have been offered up for the peculiarities of Donald Trump's speech patterns, its odd style, broken syntax, and illogic: Palilalia (involuntary repetition), a fourth-grade vocabulary, some psychological condition or other, an information-processing disorder, confabulation rather than lying, ignorance on subject matter pursuant to dyslexia, ADHD leading to the inability to stay on point, and so on. Other Presidents, such as Reagan, Eisenhower, and George W. Bush were also guilty of weird-sounding pronouncements—Reagan's sentences did not always parse, ending up far from where they started, Bush often made conclusions by repeating the premise altered slightly, and Eisenhower spouted tautologies like, "Where would this country be without this nation of ours?" Some of Warren Gamaliel Harding's speech was so strange and meandering that H. L. Mencken dubbed it Gamalielese.

Somehow I think the matter is fairly simple. The things that maddens most observers are the loose relationship that Trump's statements have with the truth, the shifting arguments, the see-through lies, the transference of responsibility, the projection of blame. However, it can be seen like this. The Trumps lived in Queens, but his father was a builder in Brooklyn. At the risk of offending the Brooklynese, I think this has something to do with it. His father was wealthy but not like the denizens of Brooklyn Heights. He came up from nothing, and he was in construction. This is what Donald grew up with, construction projects and construction workers, some of whom came from neighborhoods like Red Hook, sixty years ago places with vibrant street life, a genial way of saying that it was the boulevard of broken dreams.

Playgrounds and schoolyards are full of kids trying to get over on their mates and stay one-up. This social outlook has a particular kind of patter associated with it. The standards are not necessarily truth and fiction, but winning and losing. In one-upmanship, the truth only has meaning as a ploy. When it works in the game, you use it. Otherwise, you come up with something else. If you can say the same thing twice and mean something different the second time, you try that. Anything to get over, whether it is confusing your opponents, getting something out of them, pretending you are what you are not, or dodging trouble, that is what you do.

When you grow up this way, it is part of your developmental nature. You may move on to a boarding school because your parents came into some money, but you carry the game with you. It works in every rough-and-tumble venue like sports and dating and "the dozens"…and politics. It stays with you, even if it becomes inappropriate, because it is second nature, and other people cannot beat you at it if their only motivation is to make sense. The game is not about sense. Getting over is its *modus operandi*. The marks are any people who want to make sense.

<u>Hitler</u>

In the nascent Trump era, it has already come time to lay off the Hitler references, not that there are no reasons to bring him up or that the lessons of his perfidy have no parallels today. I have spent a lifetime studying Hitler without specializing in it or making me different from a million others or giving me any insight to offer that the world is deficient in.

It ties in with a study I began at New College a thousand years ago, and the interest never left me. My first independent study subject was the Outsider (which was how Hitler started) through the lens of Albert Camus and the Absurd. The next one was to be on messianic movements and millenarianism to explore the social mechanics: is leadership a function of the individual or does it spring from some element in the culture? As it turns out, the question of the Outsider rises up immediately, as most millenarian movements to recover lost glory have been led by figures who have internalized cultural confusion, as the Austrian outcast Hitler exemplifies. I would have gone on from this to study the American anti-hero in film and literature: the lonely cynic battles the irrational in the shadowy reaches of society and hopes to stave off being beat up long enough to make sense of things.

It turns out that I am still studying these subjects, because they are in me. I have internalized them as objects in my own psyche and refer to them unwittingly in the times I find myself wandering in the gray light when the signposts of the soul are hard to read. "Oh yes, this is what that resembles. I've seen it before."

In a roundabout way, this is why I bring up Hitler. Obviously I did not live through the mania, but I have relatives who did not live because of it. What has to be understood about Hitler, aside from the success, which did not happen for no reason, and the failure, which was inevitable for any number of reasons, is that from the time he came to a little power, he was first and foremost a prophet of violence. He was a spokesperson for and promoter of a gang of killers. In the couple of years before he was imprisoned in 1924, he was party to three hundred and fifty murders. For the next ten years, the Nazis conducted war against the Communist Party and against punitive operations mounted by the Allied powers to recover WWI reparations in default. The military missions were accompanied by more assassinations and murders in the dozens, hundreds, I doubt anybody knows the count. How Hitler ended up was how he started, drenched in blood running with killers. Real, red blood. Running in the streets. Real murderers. There is nothing we have in this country now that is anything like it.

<u>The Volunteer Psychological Panel</u>

The panel of mental health professionals volunteering to remove the President on psychological grounds of unfitness to perform is still out there lobbying to have their program confirmed. It seems that they feel their opinion is not only worth considering but also a mandatory deliberation.

Part of this problem, and it is a problem, is that they have the cart in front of the horse. Were a President to be removed on the basis of fitness, that is, the lack thereof, it would happen something like this: Somebody notices that the President does not seem to be himself. He shaves with his toothpaste and brushes his teeth with shampoo. At breakfast he starts speaking in tongues. He puts his socks on over his shoes, and he takes a golf club to everything on his desk. The people in charge bring in some Quack-in-Chief, and he puts his hand on his chin and says, well, it appears that the old man has logus of the bogus and we must put him under observation. In the meantime the VPOTUS will take over his duties.

It would not come about through the gratuitous observations of outsiders, no matter how sincere they are and how urgent is their hand-wringing, and it should not. They are welcome to mutter their incantations and quote from their manuals but beyond that, they are bystanders, unwilling though they may be to warm the bench.

A few people have found my opinion onerous, and they are welcome to that too. It has been implied that I have not received the professional divine wisdom yet, and that if I did, I would agree. This is an ancient and venerable intellectual dodge, but dodgy it is, as it was when the first Sophist to try it on for size liked how it fit.

I do not agree and will never agree. The idea that a volunteer panel of experts could remove a sitting President on the basis of a consensus opinion of his mental health is not only wrong-headed but dangerous. I say this because I do understand what they are trying on for size, and I disagree that it is a good idea. It is worse in the degree that it might be successful because it reduces the Constitution to a self-help guidebook.

We already have enough of that crap from the people in power, with their half-baked critique of the administrative state, sophomoric appeal to restructuring, banal notions of American nationalism, xenophobia disguised as a security standard, insincere populism, and protectionism masquerading as job security. For them, the Constitution is a list of suggestions, and the balance of powers in co-equal branches of government means that each branch does its own thing and stays out of the way of the others when it does not actually defy them, like estranged siblings in a dysfunctional family.

Russia and Trump

Gossip in Moscow, according to some reporters who have been there in the past few days, is that the Kremlin has the shivers over Donald Trump. Buyer's remorse is uncommon in Russian history, and the Russians are deficient in coping mechanisms for it. They had never thought that Trump would win the election. Appararently they assumed that their election machinations would be forgotten in a Clinton White House. Their basic intent was long-range, a comprehensive destabilization of the West in order to boost Russia's chances at world power.

This was known to the intelligence arms of the Obama White House, to the degree that there was talk in the summer of 2016 concerning known cyber-infiltration and possible influence-peddling by the Russians at the behest of the Kremlin. There was a security debate in the White House whether or not to launch an investigation. The President decided against it, on the theory that it would be imprudent to conduct an investigation in the middle of a Presidential campaign. He, like everybody else, thought Hillary would win, and he would kick the can down the road to her to deal with at her pleasure.

Then Trump won, and he did what Donald J. Trump does best (after bilking financial backers out of their dough). He started shooting off his mouth. The madness and chaos unnerved the Kremlin. In Russian society generally, mental illness is a stigma. It is considered shameful. Moreover, the Soviet Union leadership was very conscious of the harmful role played by mental illness in the Russian aristocracy that they had replaced. Although brutal, inflexible, and demanding, the Communists justified everything they did with a logic that was thoroughgoing, if a little weak on elegance and philosophic rigor.

This was basically how the Soviet government ruled for seventy years, cold-blooded, methodical, inefficient and tiresome, implacably resolute, the slow clenching of the iron fist and ruthless atomization of the working class even if it harmed the state.(As it did when Stalin dispossessed the Ukrainian kulaks, and the Soviet Union was never again self-sufficient in food production.) A state such as this does not tolerate madness any more than it does dissent. It has no use for the unpredictable. Neither does the state that supplanted the Soviet regime. The current kleptocracy, a conspiracy of thieves, has little tolerance for friends who stray from the plan, whatever it is, and babble nonsense. Crooks are notably single-minded in their misdemeanors. This is why they have no idea which scheme they need to handle the Trump problem of the moment: run shamelessly, pretend that it is a chimera, or double down on the destabilization plan.

MARCH....

<u>The</u> <u>Long-form</u> <u>Destabilization</u> <u>Campaign</u>

Subterfuge by foreign powers striking at the heart of American sovereignty are as rare as they are unwelcome.

It is safe to say that most Americans were surprised when they learned of the Russian interventions in the 2016 Presidential campaign. Whether or not the Russians succeeded in what they set out to do vis-à-vis the election is still an unsettled question, but it is fair to say that their true motivation would come as a shock. The Russians were not targeting the election so much. Their intention was longer-range than that, nothing less than destabilizing the representative governments of the western alliance. At the moment, how it will shake out is anybody's guess.

As rare as it is, however, the last time a foreign power mounted a long-form destabilization campaign against the American government, it lasted for twenty years, and it has been so well forgotten that when it is mentioned, the kneejerk response is an unbelieving squint and involuntary exclamation: "Hunh?" At the time, however, it made perfect sense, and the American people understood its purpose insofar as they knew, while the federal government took its rage out mainly on innocents, using many means that we now identify with totalitarian governments like the

Soviet Union. In the end the campaign was largely unsuccessful and failed to accomplish any significant destabilization. Some of it was delusional and fantastic, encompassing plot lines cut out of comic opera, and characters that Moliere and Balzac would be proud to have invented, but it was horrible and damaging too. Except for the low loss of life, the worst incident rivals any modern act of terror.

I am speaking of the destabilization campaign envisioned and acted on by the German Empire under Kaiser Wilhelm from the end of the 19th century to the end of the First World War. It was at a time when the Prussians were beginning to realize that the utility of war for profit was coming to an end, and the German search for colonial conquests overseas was ramping up. Feeling squeezed by *de jure* French and English colonialism, and by the *de facto* economic colonialism of the Americans, the Kaiser gave up on Realpolitik, the art of the possible, and turned his attention to Weltpolitik, the lust for colonial dominion. In this regard, he invested a fortune on the Imperial Navy and set out ambitious goals for German power outside the Continent.

In fact, as documents discovered in the 1930's and then decades later in German archives demonstrate, the comprehensive campaign included plans to invade the United States at the turn of the 20th century. Between 1897 and 1906 three plans were developed and abandoned in turn.

Kaiser Wilhelm knew better than to challenge either the British or the French fleets directly, so the first elements in the American destabilization campaign were skirmishes against the American Navy in the Philippines and the Caribbean during the Spanish-American War. Nothing came of these engagements, which in some respects were more like maneuvers, or impromptu war games. Germany did not give up its ambitions in Latin America, however. It had strong ties to Mexico politically, informal interests in South America owing to strong commercial trade and shipping. It was party to an international dispute in 1902 with Venezuela involving other nations, who demanded remuneration from the Venezuelan government over trade issues. When the Venezuelan government refused, and the German Navy moved against Venezuela, TR ordered the American Navy to intervene, and Germany backed down. It still attempted to establish naval bases in Puerto Rico or Cuba, and kept up a running anti-America propaganda campaign in South America, which was already fertile ground for anti-American sentiment, so in some ways it is difficult to tell how successful it was in preaching to the choir. Further efforts at propaganda inside the United States largely constituted a laughable failure.

All through this period, and unknown to the rest of the world, the Germans were hatching plans to invade the United States, either directly or after establishing naval bases by force in Puerto Rico or Cuba to use as staging areas. Germany under the Kaiser was interested in commercial ties to and control of areas of the undeveloped world that the United States considered its domain. The Germans had come late to what is called the empire race, the drive by the industrial powers to control the rest of the world, and wanted to make up for lost time. Germany was not even unified until 1871. By attacking American interests, Germany hoped to avoid the direct military confrontation that encroachment on British and French colonies would inspire.

The national grand strategy was formed as early as 1889, and its the control unit was known as Abteilung IIIb. Originally a counter-intelligence department of the military, it expanded in nature into a comprehensive plan to catch up with the British, the French, and the Americans. After skirmishes with the Americans in the South Pacific, the first plan to invade the United States in 1897 was initiated. The objective was to end up in control of the Caribbean by opening bases in Cuba and Puerto Rico, making the invasion of the United States at Newport News in Virginia and the Portsmouth naval station in New England a diversion. The second plan was to establish a base in Cuba and use it as a staging area to invade New York and Boston. It was all a fantasy, since the Germans would not have been able to muster up the ships to transport the one hundred thousand soldiers needed. By the time the third invasion plan was cooked up, the Germans and the Americans had already come into conflict in the Philippines and Venezuela over commercial interests and control of the territorial seas. The German plan was to invade Massachusetts and take Boston by landing at Provincetown and Rockport, impound the island of Puerto Rico and threaten the Panama Canal, then under construction, hoping to force the American government into negotiations over the Caribbean and South America. This was 1906, the American government had overtaken the Germans in naval strength, and the plans to invade the United States were all discarded.

Throughout this period, millions of Germans emigrated to the United States. They were the largest single immigrant population and at one point nearly ten per cent of the American population were German immigrants or descendants of German immigrants. The Germans were part of the progressive movement in American politics and were successful commercially. They were assimilating into American society.

Most of the foreign propaganda in the United States up to the First World War was British, trying to rally the Americans to British commercial trade, such as tobacco, and to stifle the Germans attempting to warn Americans off the power of the British banks. Neither British attempts were very successful. At the same time, German commercial interests in South America spread propaganda about the dangers of American ties, an issue that was easy to press in a Latin America that felt exploited by the United States. As war came closer and closer to reality, the German propaganda in the United States became more anti-British, and the British propaganda more anti-German. The American Germans grew more and more nervous, as American propaganda against them increased. In time, their anxiety proved well-founded.

At the outset of the war, the Americans were not interested in participating. As the German government continued its sabotages in the United States, directed as they were by the German diplomatic corps, sentiment in the government against Americans of German descent increased, and many were interned for little or no reason. When the Mare Island munitions dump off the coast of New Jersey was blasted to smithereens, a seismic jolt that was felt from Maryland to Rhode Island, and it was thought to be German sabotage, the sentiment against the German nation eventually turned negative enough to commit troops to the European war. At the same time thousands of ethnic Germans were interned in prisons.

The feelings against German-Americans were a long time healing, and against the German nation they did not actually recover until the Nazis were defeated in World War II.

Backward or Forward

One way to look at the current deep political division in the United States, and maybe the best way, is to see how it reflects the economic crisis caused by the dislocations of the Great Recession. At the moment this is a development question, what to do first, how to allocate money, and which people to support. The issue is national strategy.

It is clear that, privately, the money question has been settled. The financial system has been centralized. Out of the many came the few. The collapse of the savings and loans in the eighties led to the centralization of mortgage monies, the deregulation of investment banking through the repeal of the Glass-Steagal Act led to the distillation of finance to the large banks and the hedge funds, and the re-introduction of exotic financial instruments like credit-default swaps in combination with mortgage bundling led to the diversion of risk away from the loan originators. At the moment it is never clear who exactly is responsible for what, although it is clear that clever operators end up with big money.

The social question is easier to answer. Who has done well and who has not? Empirically the answer is plain. Income and wealth has risen to the top, income inequality has regressed to levels unseen since prior to World War Two after decades of leveling out, and the divide breaks down in the most striking pattern between super-city urban and small-city rural. Each of these two has its own income disparities, but the economic quandary consists in which sector to develop first, the forward section or the backward one.

Every developing economy has faced this dilemma, and the answer is not just an economic one. Originally the United States chose to develop the backward areas first, the choice of Jefferson over Hamilton, but in the end it did not work, and it took the Whigs to fashion the combination of federal spending for public works, the promotion of business, and the redress of social inequality to develop the economy. Those countries who followed the original American example of developing the backward areas first, such as China, Mexico, Brazil, and India, eventually turned away from it and developed the forward areas to come into the modern world.

In this country now, it is not at all clear what the Administration's aims are. There are signs in both directions. The friends in investment banking, technology, and defense speak to advancing the forward areas, but the Made-in-America sloganizing, the rural vote that put Trump over the top, and the promise to rebuild the Rust Belt are signals of bringing up the backward areas. If history is a guide, the forward areas come first, no matter what the sales pitch says.

Congressman Steve King and Culture

If Iowa Congressman Steve King is an epitome of American culture, that pinnacle of Western civilization we all know and love, then Western civilization is in a heap of trouble, not because Steve King is a bad person or stupid or out of touch or mean-spirited or any of the other spiny adjectives that would stick to him like magnets if you threw them at him in the dark. It is because he is so pusillanimous that he believes a few brown babies will bring Western civilization to its knees, and he is scared that his people will be forgotten for their great goodness when their shabby cowardice is actually the thing that is showing through the worn-out fabric of
The perfect life, the big lie, the dream that never fades,
The bill of goods that sells a million,
The polish set with tarnish built in,
So you always knew to bring the cloth out again,
Their God, their savings, their guns to keep
The banks afloat. They won the culture war
But winning was not good enough.
They wanted to be right, to be pretty.
The game was rigged but the prize
Was not enough. They wanted applause,

The theater of it, the cheering, brass bands,
They wanted to be boring but they wanted boredom
To be interesting, applauded, celebrated,
For boredom is their paradise and everything the same,
The way God wants in God's country. Two by two
The little creatures in the ark, the safe place,
That great good place in the mind colors the world
All bright and beautiful, the wash that kaleidoscopes
The drab and dull and ordinary with the splendor
Of the phony, the fake, the chintzy
Pretending that it is real silk satin in a marble bed.
And there they are, back in bed with the surrealists
They had cast off. Ah, what strange bedfellows
Delusion makes!

Problem <u>in</u> the <u>White</u> House

There is a problem in the White House, a big problem. A huge problem high up in the White House, but it is not the one that is being reported. It is the basis, however, for the problems that have been bothering those who have been bothered, the majority.

The problem, believe it or not, stems from bad logic. This bad logic comes from the attempt to reconcile two conflicting propositions. The first proposition is the populism of the President. According to him, he is here to help the people. This may be a sham, but it is still the fundamental proposition. He fancies himself a savior.

The second proposition is the anarchism, technically the syndicalism, of Steve Bannon. According to him, the President is here to gut the State, eviscerate the administration. This is the meaning of the obscure phrase, "deconstruction of the administrative state." Bannon fancies himself a philosopher.

How do you run a State without a government? That is to say, how do you run a state with skeleton controls in every department but the military and the security apparatus? You rule by decree. This is the polar opposite of consent of the governed. It is not governing. It is ruling.

How do you rule a State for which you claim soteriology, the salvation of the people? There are three solutions, one in theory, and two in practice as we speak. The theoretical solution goes back to 1891, when Pope Leo published his famous encyclical "De Rerum Novarum." In it he proposed an organization of society into vertical associations. The blazon for this theory is "Faith, Flag, and Family," i.e. vanilla fascism under the Catholic Church. The Trumpish formula would exclude the Church and sound more like "Country, Cash, and Cronies."

The other two possibilities are the Russian Federation and Iran. When Ruhollah Khomeini became the Grand Ayatollah of Shi'i Islam, he was wildly popular on the street, having spent years as a radio evangelist broadcasting from Iraq. He lied about it on air, but his social theory was that everyone should believe the same thing, and his political theory was that the people are wards of the state.

The Russian Federation is ruled by Vladimir Putin, who is wildly popular. He believes that the Russians are a great people who have been shuffled illegitimately to the margins of history. He believes in top-down power, his own bank account, the projection of military power, and the inherent weakness of democratic forms. He thinks the government's duty is to support the people with the kind of socialism practiced by the Somozas in Nicaragua, the "soup-bone theory of governing." Throw the soup-bones to the dog, and the dog will love you.

APRIL……..

<u>Trump the Asshole</u>

Civilization is learned behavior. This is not news.

No matter what you think of Donald Trump, whether you see him as well-acculturated or maladjusted, whether you are for him or against him, find him rude or hilarious, consider him intelligent or average, a good or bad businessman, you will be forced to agree by virtue of his own words and deeds that what he has learned about civilization is the conflict model of society. He does not appeal to conformism. He does not believe that everyone will make it. He does not believe that all people are the same under the skin.

It has been said over and over again that he loves chaos. Conflict is his friend. This has been praised and it has been deprecated. He ran for President to shake things up, and he has succeeded.

Let us not be deceived, however, where he learned this behavior. It is a common element of predatory capitalism. Competition signifies the conflict model of social change. It is so common that it is identified by some as co-terminous with capitalism. Those who fail to fight for success are losers, and therefore by comparison those who succeed are winners. This was certainly the view of the robber barons, the monopolists, the corporatists, and the social Darwinists. Your worth to society is proven by the size of your bank account.

What goes hand in hand with this is the management style of fear. If you want your people to work hard every day, you make them scared for their jobs, you confuse them to see how they will react, and you set them against each other to see who will win out. Many inferior managers use this style because it suits them, many do it because it is easy, and many do it because it satisfies their need to have power over others. It works. Otherwise it would not be practiced so often.

They are the ideas, however, that appeal to the hard drivers and the swelled heads, the people who want to prove to themselves that they are great, as well as the ones who think that they were born great. They can always prove that they are great at making others uncomfortable and getting over that way. In other words, if you claim to be an asshole, you can always prove it at any given moment.

At any given moment, Donald Trump can always prove it. Whether you think it is a good thing or not, you have to agree. He has carved this little piece of history out for himself. You have to give him that.

Or you can follow the advice of Larry Fine, him of the Three Stooges: "If at first you don't succeed, suck until you do suck seed."

<u>To a Critic Who Shall be Nameless to Protect Him</u>

It was difficult to figure out how to approach this subject of your tendentious and juvenile harangues. Should I respond in kind or take the high road?

Should I consider Marx, unable to disentangle the sentiment from the analysis, conflating the normative argument against capitalism's perfidies so hopelessly with the pragmatic report of its shortcomings that no coherent politico-economic thesis could possibly eventuate? In brief, Edmund Wilson's criticisms of Marx?

Or should I think in terms of Isaiah Berlin and his foxes and hedgehogs? Widely represented now as the difference between big-picture and detail orientation, this is a mild perversion of what he actually said. The hedgehogs, whether they are detail-oriented or not, are interested in close analysis what goes wrong. The foxes take a stand and go with it, whether they understand the big picture or not.

This line did not satisfy the need to account for the blustering and posturing and gratuitous disdain. So then I thought maybe it would be instructive to reflect on Tolstoi and Dostoevski.

Tolstoi understood everything he knew about history, insofar as he did know about history, in minute detail he could bring to mind and grapple with as if playing a game. It was a large game with consequences, but a game nonetheless, animated by passion but directed with cold reason. He understood everything but the broad sweep of it.

Dostoevski, on the other hand, was all instinct and hunger, directed at many of the same subjects as Tolstoi but without the attentive temper. He was Mikhail Mikhailov's tortured writer looking for relief from pain in the Church or George Steiner's revolutionary apostate whose battle with the State was only a metaphor for the battle with God. God takes no prisoners. God settles it. One obeys or suffers. It was no accident whom Dostoevski befriended, Pobedonostsev, architect of the Pale and one of history's arch-villains, the Grand Inquisitor made flesh.

This makes sense for your displaced rage and supercilious insults, comic enough to evoke Yosemite Sam, and so puerile it demeaned the speaker more than the target, but the mark twain had yet to be sounded. This was the part hardest to figure out, the hapless spite coupled with the pompous blore. It was the Wizard of Oz gone apoplectic, a little man in a big mask too heavy to bear, threatening destruction when he could barely maintain the decibel level.

.

A tragic monologue without the tragedy. Comedy unintended, in other words, bathos.

<u>FLY</u> <u>THE</u> <u>BLUE</u> <u>THE</u> <u>DOVE</u>

If in the window fly the blue the dove
Wing on the wind the scent of lavender
Despair denied and off the clouds the rain
Falls out and pelts the dirt with screaming love
The flowers bend and weep and drink the pain
And rise in pride that locates golden sun
What wonder give the flavor to it all
When shadow fall and sweet old respite run

The course grown tall the weeds the dreams the crawl
The marbled seascape where shining splendor
Soars low and licks the waves the nightmares prey
Above. So hard the sunlight seems a day
Too late and nothing solved. At last the blue
The open window follows. The dove too.

PLEASE REMIND THE DIRT

If you solve the night you still have the day
To fix and not vice-versa. Screwing
A light bulb in a socket does nothing
The yard needs. The bony fingers of death beckon.
Who cares? The flowers? Please remind the dirt
The reaper does not cut his fingernails
Nor daisies. The breezes bend to the will
Of the dandelion. The grim one's pen
Ran out of ink, so long, so long ago.
He writes on chaff, sleeps on mulch, breaks his fast
In silence. Nothing to speak of speaking
About. Bored to tears. Worse for that. Rises.
Points a skinny finger at the roses.
The lilies stand still like soldiers at ease.
The rake waits patiently. The hooded one
Must turn the sun off, shuffles on weary,
So much time and so little good to do.

MAY..........

<u>Regarding DNA, Ethnicity, and Science</u>

Knowledge and fallacies brought about by the controversy over Elizabeth Warren's case.

The first thing to be said about ethnicity is that we know it as a social grouping, the empirical evidence of people who live together, speak the same language, hold customs in common, marry and have children. Organized in various kinds of kinship groupings, hierarchies, networks, and associations, people identify as in-group and out-group and keep records, either oral histories or otherwise, of who they are and how they are related.

Thus, the initial mode of inquiry is to find out who is related to whom according to how they identify themselves. Who are the Cherokee and what do they say about themselves? Beside their culture, in what ways are they alike morphologically? What are their body types, sizes, skin color, blood type, etc? And what are the variations and their distribution?

After this is done, then genetic materials derived according to physical variations can be typed. To do this, complete individual genomes must be decoded and mapped to find the range of genomes and develop a typical range of genetic attributes. This is how the typical genome is developed. The question can then be asked how closely an individual genome matches the typical genome. What markers in the typical genome are found in the individual genome? Then an unknown sample can be decoded and mapped to determine how it compares to the typical genome. To be scientific and comprehensive, the entire sample genome must be studied.

In other words, in order to codify an unknown genome, the known genome must have been identified absolutely. This is not an economic means of determining genealogy by DNA analysis. Therefore statistical analysis is required to compare certain critical genetic markers. This is indicative but not dispositive. The pie-charts used to sell DNA kits on television are not nearly as accurate as depicted, although they are simple and suggestive.

The other relatively simple way to determine whether someone has some relation to some ethnic group is to examine the marriage records and see if the right names crop up. This may not be easy, and it may be time-consuming, but it does not require elaborate expensive equipment and advanced degrees. On this score Elizabeth Warren has near-zero probative evidence that there are Cherokee, or Delaware, in her bloodline. This method has its own drawbacks, however. Many persons in 19th century Oklahoma, such as Warren's forebears, did not claim native heritage because of shame and discrimination.

If, however, a complete DNA scan is performed and typed scientifically, a completely different outcome may come about.

The discrepancy between the two methods cannot be demonstrated at the moment, because the complete genome analyses have not been performed, either for Cherokee or generalized Native American. The gaps have been filled, where they have been filled, by digital statistical analysis, high-grade mathematics whose databases may or may not be sufficient to produce an unimpeachable answer.

THE SCENT OF LILY

Waiting for the old man to catch me up
Is not so long as it is tedious.
The tedium is instantaneous
Like the white on the lily of the vale.
It starts where it is and ends there also
Family of the dirt and no moving on.
And when the sunshine grows low on the swale
My brother the dirt will cover me. Gone

The old man sowing grief on tip-toe,
Shy to wake the smilers eager to sup
With the devil and carouse the night down
To the bare nub of it, when nary a frown
Betrays the hint of subtle misery,
Tender, fleeting as the scent of lily.

LA CONJUGACIÓN DE LA VEJEZ

No puedo. Me matará, ese flan
De pudín tan suave, tan dulce,
Tanto fino, tonto rico. A mí me daña
El azucar, el amor, la garantía de la dulzura
Eternal. Clamo yo que fluctuan
El tiempo, que el clima sea borrascoso
Cuando, cuando, cuando
No es portátil el sentido perenne,
Bien desesperado. Es una idiotez,
A pensar que el sombrio pase
Fácil al júbilo. No soy un idiota,
Sin duda depende en lo cual gozo
Me ofrezca cuando que estoy perezoso,
Naturalmente. No se puede.
La iluminación de los dioses
No me cubre la cabeza
Por la conjugación de la vejez.
Todos los milagros ya se me vayan.

<u>THE</u> <u>CONJUGATION</u> <u>OF</u> <u>OLD</u> <u>AGE</u>

I cannot. It will kill me, this bread custard
So soft, so sweet, so very fine, silly rich.
I am hurt by the sugar, the love, the guarantee
Of eternal sweetness. I clamor for the weather
To fluctuate, for the climate to be a tempest
When, when, when it is not portable
The perennial sense, fully desperate.
It is an idiocy to think that the gloom
Would pass easily to jubilation.
I am not an idiot, without doubt
Depending on which pleasure
You offer me when I am idle,
Naturally. It is not possible.
The illumination of the gods
Does not cover my head for me
On behalf of the conjugation of old age.
All the miracles would go away from me now.

CERULEAN SKY

It was a cerulean sky tonight.
I think cerulean is the right word,
The color of a shallow mountain lake
When the sun is overhead,
Pale but saturated, with puffball clouds
Scudding past to the east
And a pale orange wash where the sun
Just left. Venus so bright it was making
The crescent moon shine all by its lonesome.
It stayed that way a long time, the whole way
To the library. Here at the confluence
Of the Anacostia and the Potomac
The sky is rarely clear like this,
And it never stays when it is.
I saw it for the first time this night.
Funny how this happens
Where you have been
So many times before.
It feels like prayer.

LAVENDER SKY

It was a lavender sky tonight,
an intense band of pale violet
trending from open sky blue
to a wall of bar harbor gray
at the eastern horizon.
The lilac lasted ten seconds,
no more, in electric mood
and softened up, a wash, a dim reminder
of glory. You had to be looking at it first
to see it. There was no looking away
and catching it before it dissolved.
Half a world over, the horizon band
was pure sweet tangerine. It stayed
and stayed and stayed and stayed
and lingered in the afterglow.

THE <u>WIND</u> IS <u>STILL</u> UPON US

The winter's gray wind is still upon us,
The endless beating on the window panes,
The ceaseless howling 'tween the building walls,
The constant clacking of the trees' branches,
Brown leaves flying the air without sound wings
And crows mis-judging their perches, hanging
From one foot a tick before letting go,
The gulls bulling their skinny wings ahead
Until it catches up and flings them back
And up a hundred yards all akimbo
And looking like casualties in a war
Shot through with BB's and yet no blood.
Off they shoot the other way, just like you
When it cries screaming through your battered soul
After the night's black dogs put wet noses
On the back of your neck in the deep dark
And the lone stand against the enemy
Within who holds you in his arms, his hands
Stroking your hair, him who is you, not-you
And everything else and who flies the air
On wings you grew and winds you made and skies

You conjured up for lack of something better
To do or something worse to be scared of
Or nothing at all but what might grow there
Of its own accord, like the will of God
Growing in its own space unimpeded
And there you are, flung up and back, all sprawled
Against the wind and shot through with BB's
All akimbo and yet no blood, and yet
And yet, and yet, and yet and all alive.

ORANGE DREAMSICLE SKY

Tonight it was the orange dreamsicle sky
Just like Tom Waits predicted off the streetlights
In the far L. A. distance over the ghetto streets
From inside the diner where breakfast is served
At midnight or any night when the jukebox
Plays Nat King Cole intoning Flash! Bam!
Allakazam! Under an Orange Colored Sky
Wonderful you came by but wonderful you
Did not come by it was the orange dreamsicle sky
Half the global atmosphere albeit fading back
To cloudy white at the outer edges like the dreamsicle
Does when bit. Nor was it L. A. They do not allow
The orange dreamsicle sky in L. A.
They let in the orange haze oppressive
Like the smell of petty failure and the fake allure
With brown edges and the stink of cigarette butts
And the crazy look of the stinking crackhead
With burning cuffs and smoke roiling out
His ears and all the orange dreamsicle wrappers
Littered round his sneakers. This is not L. A.
And that is not the orange dreamsicle sky

That swept the horizon flat as a dreamsicle wrapper
Run over by a steamroller on a mission
To kill all the dreamsicle visions but the sun
Had already set and the steamroller missed its target.
And there alone the orange dreamsicle sky
Wiped the edge from end to end
But not beginning to end.
Only now in the middle.

THE RIDDLE THIS

I love you and always have. I suspect
I always will but love's a funny thing.
At times you have it and stand ignorant.
At other times you think you have it down
And all you really have is a precious
Memory of a fantasy to drown
Your sorrows in and soothe life with a rant
Against the perils of the randy sect.

Dear God, there is no meritorious
Way to want so much without offering
The sun to the flower. Follow the sun,
The riddle this in hand, not the question.
To bring the gift that has yet to exist
And offer it for free, this is the twist.

<u>DEAR</u> <u>DR.</u> <u>SCRUELEUCE:</u> <u>Chapter</u> <u>Two</u>

If I thought you were playing at being a royal horse's ass, I would applaud the performance for its craft and talent alike. I have no problem with your philosophy, except that it reads out like a theosophy in which both the specious and the spurious live side by side with the valuable, recognizing at the same time that it has more attractive coherence than, say, the perorations of Sondra London.

In any case, I do not present either my friends or acquaintances with a list of notions they must agree to in order for me to withstand their company. Frankly, what you think is no affair of mine. If your ideas were more interesting, or your outlay a little more clever than juvenile, I might find your sense of humor slightly more entertaining than Ottis Toole on an off night. As it is, however, you cannot win this little game you have created. A game requires an opponent.

Your Humble Servant.

MIDDLE OF THE NIGHT

I met him in the middle of the night.
I grappled with him then with all my might.
He threw a blow that struck me in the heart.
I woke to find my fingers round his hand
And in his hand was my hand round his own,
But his was in the center of my chest
As strong as life itself and all the rest
Came clear as hammers ringing on a stone.

I sat there waiting for my time to come
But something kept me holding on. As numb
My fingers gripping on the bed, as sand
Goes slipping through the glass, as in the art
Of dreaming goes the silence of the night
So too the wisdom of the darkness bright.

JUNE............

Hair

Let's get this over with. The real trouble with Donald Trump is
hair. This is not an assay of the perils of a suicide blonde wanting
to be President, nor is it a study of the peculiar delusions of bald
men with comb-overs, although these are both part of it. The
question is, since it is definitely not a hairpiece, what is it?

First of all, the hair is sick. It has been cooked and colored so many
times that without the spray lacquer on top and the mousse on the
sides it would lie on his pate like a fringed dragon at death's door,
gasping for breath. It is so frizzled that it looks like a straw hay-
bale left out in the sun for weeks to desiccate and has so many split
ends you would go stark staring mad getting them counted.

Then there is the color. Although inventive as many of the blonde
colors affected by glamour-baby darlings of the silver screen,
natural hair of this peach champagne color is rare as sprinting
terrapins. Certainly no seventy year old man has had hair this color
without chemical intervention. As to whether it adds the effect of
beauty, a beholder would need a tolerant eye to see it.

As to the cut, it is not too dissimilar from the last seventy year old
President with a pompadour, although Ronald Reagan's coif was a

modest step back from Elvis Presley's high pompadour of the fifties. Reagan's hair looked to be in good condition. It did not seem like a dead animal on his head. It was dyed skillfully to cover the gray, all protestations to the contrary laughable. It had actually once been his natural color (unlike Elvis, who had dyed his hair black on the way to stardom.)

Then there is the question of the method. First, three parts are made with a comb, one on each side and one in back, where the hair is about a foot long. The back hair is swept forward and spray lacquered hard, and the hair on the sides is greased and combed back. Then bits of hair are skillfully manipulated to make it look like the part is on the left and the pompadour lifts up from there. In fact the front bit is the back, rolled under slightly to conceal the split ends. The false pompadour is fixed with lacquer, converting it into one solid sheaf of hair that flaps gloriously up and down in the wind over the glabrous patch underneath.

Indeed, it looks like a marvelous construction that would make an extremely effective clown fright-wig, if the gig and costume were appropriate. Herein lies the problem. What is this spectacular hair supposed to be saying? It is certainly not normal. Could anyone who was wearing it actually think that the spectators are fooled into thinking that it is not a combover? In his presence how could anyone do anything but stare at it rudely? This is not any better way to greet a President than it is for a President to be greeted.

SPIDER SPIDER BLACK

I killed a spider black in the bathtub
Tonight I meant to save the little thing
It struggled so hard in the shower spray
And fell off the side time and time again

A tiny black flower it was after
Lying akimbo on the porcelain
The water its bed of surface tension
Trapping it all its limbs at angles

I had tried to save it from the hot spray
To let it cling to a clean brown washcloth
And then when its little legs would not move
With a tissue corner soak up the drop

Like a tiny flower crushed it lay there
And lay there when it dried like a flower

<u>Deselection of the Rational</u>

There is a set of Novocollegians, who I would guess to be in the thirty to forty-five year old range, who fit into the rational deselection pattern. Some of them are in the mode of passive hostility to baby boomers, a sentiment more common than the baby boomers want to admit.

I have noticed this subset acting out on Facebook from time to time and have engaged them, mostly without satisfaction. You can wrestle them in a toxic death match of opinions but a healthy tussle is too much to ask for.

They are genuinely hostile to science and mathematics but it is never easy to tell if the root cause is unfamiliarity or incompetence. There are two camps, one which identifies science as co-terminous with scientism, the belief that all important questions are scientific ones. These anti-scientism crusaders look on rationalism—which does indeed have its limitations—as a religious devotion preventing other means of divining the truth. They believe that arguing against you is a necessary precaution against the pounding fist of scientism dogma, even if you are only making a mild defense of secular rationalism.

The other camp sees mathematics as a kind of casting of spells. This group takes statistics, for example, as a counting up of data and subtracting one set from the other to arrive at an arithmetic positive. This is the fact to them. The resulting percentage is taken as a hard number. Introducing the concept of "standard deviation from the mean" they consider merely a way to muddy the water.

To them, the probability of a particular coin toss is $n/2$, pure and simple, and you're only going to get them mad explaining a standard deviation from the mean, that a pure 50/50 chance out of a hundred tosses is an unlikely outcome, by dint of probabilities. Exactly five million heads and five million tails out of ten million tosses seems improbable if one thinks about it, but 5.01 million over 4.99 million out of 10 million seems easy to understand. The farther out you go, the closer the theoretical 50% approaches, but the actual equation is $n/2$ plus or minus the square root of n, except when it is three or smaller. Chew on that apple for a moment. Truly, there are many ways to abuse statistics, but the standard deviation is rarely one of them.

JULY..............

The Plot to Hack America

Let's pretend that the tale has the Americans being the grifters and the Russians being the accomplices. Let's guess that this narrative has flaws in it. Then just for fun, let's imagine that the Russians were the ones who blew the game, and the Americans are running scared because they thought they were working with professionals, not a gang of careless kvass-drinking boobs who were uncool and heavy-handed. Let's also say that the reason the Americans didn't know any better was that they themselves were uncool, heavy-handed boobs, without the kvass.

To be good, this hacking bit was supposed to be done on the down low, secret as only secret can be. If it is done in secret, professionally, then finding out who did it takes experts of a high degree of skill and determination to figure out how it was done. To make a comparable example, if professionals conduct a clandestine search of your abode, everything is left exactly as it was. Exactly, so that you can't tell right away.

If you say, naw, the hackers can't have been so stupid as to leave a digital trail to follow, or worse, talk to the client in trackable form or out in the open on a phone, the easy answer is well, yes they can. The Russians have never had the reputation of being slick. In fact, some of their sarcastic comments on the hacking expertise reflect this. Putin and Julian Assange both said that any teenage computer hacker could have done most of it, because the data had not been firewalled. It's also hard to believe that the fake news on social media that accompanied the hacking could be accomplished without American help. If this were true, we would have hordes of Russians writing sit-com scripts.

We also know that the Russian oligarchs are not notable for their subtlety but for their ostentation and ham-handed power-grabbing. These are the guys we're accusing of being too slick for words? This could be the same thing that the Americans involved in the hacking are saying to themselves now: "These are the guys we trusted to get it right? What the hell were we thinking?"

THE EIGHTH

Clothing is a Tell

In card play, a "tell" is an unconscious give-away from a player what he holds in his hand. It is almost impossible for an amateur to control his tells. He may be completely unaware that he has them.

Other signs of life have tells. Clothing has tells that hide psychology. Trump and Putin have conspicuous sartorial tells. They have the same one. Not everybody notices these right away. People who are in the trade and their families do. These people encounter the issues on a daily basis. My father's father was a tailor, and my father was a dry cleaner who also sold custom mail-order suits.

Some men require a suit coat conforming to an image that does not match the body they actually have. They want the coat shoulders broader than their own, to give an impression of strength and confidence and athleticism. In order to do this, the pads inside the shoulders are built up and stiffened to maintain a straight line. This kind of exaggerated shoulder construction makes it obvious, when the man sits with his arms forward, that the garment is a kind of theatrical costume. The coat shoulders are decoration, a psychological statement, vanity, yet neither Trump nor Putin is conspicuously narrow-shouldered, simply somewhat rounded.

Why do they need the built-up pads? The square cut is done for a man who is more or less deeply insecure, who has to demonstrate he is superior because he feels inferior on account of rounded edges. Such a man does indeed have a problem.

About Trump and Putin, this was clear as day as the two of them sat talking in Hamburg. It signifies that both of them are uneasy about their physical stature (and also that they want to deny it.) It is telling that they have their coats cut to give the appearance of shoulders more square than they have. Who else but them actually cares about the size and shape of their shoulders? Most people pay no attention to trivia like this. Clothing is supposed to fit. The public does not notice when it has smooth lines.

They do notice when the fit is awkward, disheveled, full of deep wrinkles from outsize shoulder pads, even though they may not realize why or what the motivation is. Or what it tells them about the man in the coat with the phony shoulders. It tells them that he is trouble.

Clothing makes the man, the saying goes. It unmakes the man, too.

<u>Ethic and Ethics, general note on the uses of, grammatically, and how to construct an appropriate sentence on a current topic, accordingly:</u>

1. The noun Ethics is generally singular when it denotes the science or philosophy of morality, or the relationship between axiology (the study of values) and deontology (the study of obligations.) — "Ethics is a field that comes in several variations."

2. The noun Ethics is usually plural when it indicates the rules or standards of a particular calling or profession, which almost always appears with it as a qualifier. — "Legal ethics are different from political ethics."

3. The noun Ethic is singular by definition, and it always refers to a world-view or set of standards on norms of behavior not limited to ethics questions per se.—"The Protestant work ethic has been supplanted to some degree by a Wall Street ethic of greed." (It is, I suppose, possible to use the noun in the plural to lump together or collate a number of different cultural ethics but this is seldom seen. The syntax would be recast to avoid confusion. "More than one ethic" or "different varieties of ethic" or so on and so forth.)

The word Ethic is not generally used to signify one sample of a list of Ethics as in Definition 2., and Ethics does not generally denote a list from which a particular Ethic can be picked. Normally the component parts are presented as Issues-and-Standards or Questions-and-Rules or something else similar, like Norms-and-Strategies. Breaking down the Ethics of a particular model of endeavor, such as business ethics or political ethics, often takes the form of a trouble-shooting scheme or a flow chart, and sometimes a hierarchy of importance.

The appropriate adjective is Ethical, although Ethic could possibly stand in, as in the difference between comic and comical, but it would be unusual and odd.

Using the three meanings in a sentence: "In the Trump Presidential ethic, ethics is a mode of research too lofty for the political realm, wherein the ethics of criminal apprehension are the only ones that matter."

APOLOGUE TO RICK

I have never understood why people who pick fights act surprised
when they get one. This happens often to the passive-aggressive,
because it is part of that routine and to be expected.

Every retail store clerk knows that some people come into stores
for the express purpose of picking a fight, so that they can be
outraged that they are in one. Every liquor store in the world has
them. Liquor stores attract them. For many alcoholics the argument
itself is the whole point. The issues are secondary.

The internet works the same way. One clue that the argument itself
is the point is the tendency to double down at every opportunity.
When people could easily let it go, they up the ante. This is one of
the expressions of trolling.

With you, I learned early on to let your clumsy attempts at humor
go, the ham-handed digs, the inappropriate belittling, the reaction
to poetry by evoking a comic image. This is because I figured you
for an innocuous prat in your dotage, a development I have noted
in a few of my contemporaneous friends. Finally I had had enough,
and I objected. I was not hurt, as you thought, but I still know what
a slap in the face is. Then you doubled down, a mistake because

you did not really understand the subject. I knew that you did not understand the subject, and I told you so. Your response was to triple down.

I'm not sorry for anything I said, except that when I called you an idiot, you misunderstood, apparently, that I was calling you stupid. The etymology of the "idiot" metaphor refers to someone who is in his own world, self-contained, whereas "stupid" has linguistic roots in the effect of being smacked on the head and stupefied, literally. After that, the more you aggrandized your perceived injuries, the less sympathetic I became, as you were becoming more and more self-defined.

You are none of those terrible things you thought I was saying. What you are is an ordinary man who made the mistake of thinking he could control an internet conversation by limiting it to his own standards. Your punch was not big enough to attempt a "*force majeur*", and you did not have the forensic skills to play defense.

It will not happen again. I can guarantee this.

Sense of Entitlement

I spent twenty-five years working in some of the best liquor, wine, and cigar stores in our nation's capital. Every store has shoplifting. It is nothing compared to employee theft, but still, it is not nothing.

The people shoplifting fine wine and premium cigars are men who drive Benzes, Beamers, Jaguars, and Range Rovers, doctors, lawyers, university professors, diplomats, and judges. Invariably they dress well. They have ingenious methods. They know which stores have lax security procedures. One gentleman who shoplifted all over town only stole expensive Italian wine. Others would steal good wine by the case, showing cashiers a cheap wine to charge them for twelve of. It is not easy to instruct unsavvy cashiers to stop trusting men in expensive suits.

Besides the skill and the social standing, the other way they were alike were their reactions when caught. None were ashamed, none admitted it or denied it, a few were angry, and some pled justification on whatever grounds they could dream up. One prominent doctor who was caught, told to leave and not come back, went straight to the owner and negotiated a way to shop under supervision. At a later date, we salespeople had to eject him for attempting to shoplift expensive beer.

When I told a good customer, a well-to-do sophisticate from the West Coast, he said, "I'm not surprised. When I was a kid, I worked at a fancy men's store in Palm Springs. A famous singer and actor was one of our frequent customers. Every time he came in the store, he put a silk tie in his pocket. No one ever said a thing about it. He acted like it was his. He was casual about it. Sense of entitlement."

Sense of entitlement. Owners minimize it. They call the cops on petty thieves but fail to confront wealthy amateur grifters beating them out of hundreds of dollars.

An analogy to this (without the crime) happens all the time on the internet. People who feel they have standing object to something you have, some idea, some fact; you try to get rid of them, but they want to argue. When you have out-argued or dispensed with them, they feel they are entitled to something. They feel entitled to your agreement that you were wrong and they were right. They will even argue that your idea and your fact were theirs to begin with. You cannot disabuse them of their phony notions. Any attempt to do so will only strike up another argument.

The one thing that all the social media have done is to encourage this sense of entitlement. Intellectual fraud is just a game, and there is no penalty.

<u>Is</u> <u>This</u> <u>How</u> <u>a</u> <u>Real</u> <u>Estate</u> <u>Company</u> <u>is</u> <u>Run?</u>

On MSNBC tonight, July 28, either anchor Lawrence O'Donnell or guest former George W. Bush speechwriter David Frum said, talking about the current White House, "This may be how a real estate company is run, but it is not the way any other Presidential Administration has done things." They were focusing on the f___ing Anthony Scaramucci f___ing kill-the-f___ing-leakers tantrum.

It is indeed how many real estate companies are run, including some giant ones. I have over two decades of experience in dealing with and working for real estate companies, both directly as an employee and a contractor, and indirectly as a representative of a store. At a mall space managed by the largest property management company in the world, the phone numbers to the mall office were never answered, especially the maintenance division. Security answered the phone, sometimes. The local chief executive came into the store one day, after a window had been broken during an altercation between a mall patron and security. "What happened?" he asked me. I said, "I don't know. I wasn't here. You need to ask the owners." "The owners?" he shouted. "I'm the f___ing owner."

At one real estate company where I was an employee, a large national company, we were in the process of renovating an apartment building. The nicely appointed lobby was not part of the project, and one day a property manager stormed into the office and yelled, "Somebody go tell the f___ing tenants in the lobby to get the f___ back to their apartments!" An accompanying property manager turned to me and asked, "Could we make the boiler room the prettiest boiler room in town?"

The manager for the landlord at a store where I worked was a strange, intelligent character. He dressed well, looked normal, spoke in complete sentences. He would show up unannounced, however, with paperwork to sign without giving a clear explanation why. If you mentioned mildly that you were not a secretary, and he needed to talk to an owner, he would fly into a spit-spewing rage, shouting complete nonsense intelligibly..

At another building where I was employed by the real estate company, a property manager surveilled me all day long in the performance of my duties, peeking around corners and generally acting like Peter Sellers' Inspector Clouseau. A tenant had thrown out a perfectly good electronic piano, which I moved to a storage room. At the end of the day, the property manager came up to me and said, out of the blue, "Lose the piano." It was literally the only thing he said all day.

If you think government is strange, try property management some time.

TRUMP ON LINCOLN: THE MISUNDERSTANDING

Since Donald Trump brought up Lincoln the other day, both wrongly and in ignorance, as the only President he would agree he stood second to in terms of being "Presidential," it might be good to remember the main ways in which Lincoln differs from Trump, including "Presidentiality." In fact they differ so completely that their names should only fit in the same sentence when there is a negative in it.

In the first place, Lincoln was barely Presidential in the theatrical sense that another of Trump's idols, Ronald Reagan, was thought to be Presidential: self-contained, confident, straight-shooting, and clear-eyed. At the time he was elected, Reagan had these qualities in such degree that his critics considered them all he could have, the bearing, not the actuality, from spending all his free time rehearsing. After all, he was a member of "The Profession." An actor.

Lincoln had few such slick qualities. After his election to the Presidency, he sneaked into the White House in the dead of night under heavy military guard. When William T. Sherman, whose brother John was a well-known Washington figure, first met Lincoln, he was shocked at his roughness and rude manner of speech, and Sherman himself was hardly remarkable for grace and polish. Just prior to giving the Address at Gettysburg, Lincoln was regaling onlookers behind the lectern with a ribald song, and it was suspected that he had done so under the effect of a wee dram or two. Lincoln was a strange man, occasionally given to debilitating depression.

However, he had presence and *gravitas*, and he was a true leader, intellectually generous, a gifted writer, and a man of implacable beliefs. One of those beliefs, one that he is rarely given credit for, is probably the main reason he persisted in the fight to save the Union. It was that no country should be allowed to perish in which a poor boy such as he had been, so disadvantaged and downtrodden growing up, could become its President. To Lincoln, this was the American promise. The American Dream for him was nothing like what it is today—a car, a home, a paid-up mortgage, and a retirement plan—it was the chance for the poorest of the poor to rise to the top. The Union must remain whole.

Even going into all the little ways Lincoln was deficient, the limits of his grandiose vision, or the irony of denying the South the right of self-determination, this one idea still makes him stand so far above pretenders to greatness like the overdone, crass, pompous egoist Donald Trump, that the picture defies description. Trump is a child of privilege, a man-of-the-people in name only, and a politician too ignorant to recognize his own meager standing in Presidential history.

AUGUST...............

The Power of Denial

I don't want to drag this debate out forever, and I do understand your contentions. To their discredit, the Germans themselves kicked the argument off all those decades ago by making the absurd and indefensible claim that *only the Nazi operators* knew what had happened, as in the infamous line by Marlene Dietrich to Spencer Tracy in "Judgement at Nuremberg": ***"We did not know!"*** Her character said *we*, not *I*.

I am not talking about "collective responsibility" but more like collective denial. Ortega said in Ch. 6 of <u>What is Philosophy</u>, "As the biologists say, the functions most recently acquired by a species, being higher and more complex, are more easily lost. In other words, that which is most valued is always in greatest peril. In cases of conflict, of depression, of passion we are always quick to drop intelligence." I know an entire set of intelligent people I grew up with who are racists and bigots, without question, who honestly see group fault in black people and Muslims as if it were a fact. They see white people as perfectly reasonable who use any handy means of racial suppression in suburban Missouri, such as Ferguson, because they think of themselves as unbiased. Accused of bias, they will automatically say something like, "I have black friends. I know some Muslims. I'm not against Obama because he's black and has an "ethnic" name but because he's an idiot." They are in denial about their own biases despite their intelligence, and they are in denial collectively, reinforcing each other's prejudices.

I'll come back to the psychological issue in a minute, but first it has to be understood what the collective responsibility is. In the Germany of 1933, the coalition of the left and center easily had the votes to control the Bund, and the Communist Party had the muscle to stand up to the Brownshirts. The German Communist Party had been usurped by operators from Moscow, however, and the local leaders were pushed aside or bumped off. The Soviet Communist Party's main theme was ruining all the Socialist Parties, anything that looked even remotely like co-operatives or populism. To do this, it made mock of a decade of intermittent civil war with the Nazis by cooking up a deal to stand aside on that fateful day in the Bundestag when the Brownshirts wandered the halls with billies threatening everyone with a trip to the hospital. Nazi and Communist alike had totalitarian interests and a belief in the use of the concentration camp for general social control, instead of what it had been up until that time, an expedient to deal with refugee control. The collective responsibility is the deal between the Nazis and the Communists. This was followed by massive purchases of armor from Soviet Russia, in line with the provisions of the Rapallo Treaty of 1923.

Now, to get back to the collective denial question. Information theory alone will suggest that 10-15M Germans knew about the true purpose of the concentration camp system, no one knows how much. Assuming that 175-225 thousand persons were actively involved in some hands-on capacity or other, from the Gestapo, SA, and SS down to accounting to transport to manufacture of chemicals, etc., assuming everybody has a couple of people that they confide in to some degree—wife, drinking buddy, brother, etc.—and assuming the social contagion goes six degrees out, then you end up with 2 to the 6th power + 1, or 65 people radiating out from each person involved. This is a chain of information involving eleven and a half to fourteen and half million people.

Secrets are burdens. Of course, the quality of transmitted information degrades the farther out it goes. I was surprised by your reference's estimates of thirty to fifty per cent, especially the higher number, not because it could not be true, but because it would entail a degree of contagion unlikely where it was actively suppressed. "Know" is a word with many connotations, however, and several different standards of resolution.

In the United States currently, where the information is readily available, as few as eight per cent of the people comprehend the vast, some would say disgraceful, number of people in prison and what they did to get there. Depending on what questions are asked in polls of which set of subjects, it looks like fewer than one in ten are well-informed, maybe two have a passing knowledge at best, and the other seven don't know or don't care or both. The ignorance persists despite growing publicity and changing prison demographics: less black, more white. It's an open secret: unburdening is not an issue. The role of collective denial is not known.

Obviously, if the Nazis had already been throwing ordinary Germans by the tens of thousands into unspecified detention and work camps where they were starved, beaten to death, or murdered for minor camp violations, and Mein Kampf had already told everybody what Hitler planned for non-Aryans, common sense would tell you that concentration camps were always a distinct possibility, and they would be worse. Twenty to thirty per cent saturation would be enough to cause alarm. In a non-dyadic society like Germany, where social groups limit contact with outsiders and the mutual internal trust quotient is high, the whispering would be general and constant, wondering who was going on the chopping block next. Ordinary intelligence, however, was ruled out in favor of beliefs about German character and destiny and value, and denial took over, denial that was deep and collective. They knew but the information was in conflict with their beliefs, and the reinforcement was general and social. They let their desires and fears, which come from somewhere below the cerebral cortex, over-rule the frontal lobes and the capacity for judgment.

After that, it's all double-think, knee-jerk, and goose-step. When denial knocks on the door, good sense jumps out the window.

What is it About Vladimir Putin?

Why is Vladimir Putin so important and why does he think he is so important? Are they one and the same thing?

Russia is an important nation if the Russians think it is, whatever its actual status in the world is. This is the main line of reasoning, such as it is. It is true that they have numerous nuclear weapons, and that they supply a good deal of Europe with its natural gas, and that they have a relatively large military considering their meager Gross Domestic Product, but these facts are not sufficient to base a conclusion of greatness on.

Its economy is about the size of the five boroughs of New York City. For a Russian population of a hundred and a half million, this is not exactly outstanding. It reflects better on New York than it does Russia. Neither are self-sufficient in food production, a rather more critical issue for New York, inasmuch as the where to grow it does not exist. If Russia had nothing to sell, however, the world could get along without it, although it would cause a few economic dislocations here and there. If New York City stopped producing what it produces, the entire global economy would flutter and go into a tailspin of more or less fatal severity.

Vladimir Putin is important because people are scared of him and with good reason. If you cross him, there is a fair chance you will die the death of a rag baby doll. He is wealthy and has the resources of an entire country and its excellent criminal upstarts at his disposal. In this respect, he resembles his Romanov forebear, Ivan. Not the Great. The Terrible, who was not given his nickname as many think, for the depredation of his enemies on the battlefield, but for the terrible things he did to people he knew, including his family.

The Russian thugocracy is operating a kind of protection racket. If you do not agree that we are a great and powerful nation, they say, we will find a way to make you hurt. We will devote a great deal of attention to find ways to make you hurt, because we feel that we are great, and we demand that you feel this way too.

Vladimir Putin wants respect, and if he is unable to get it any other way, he will simply step on you until he finds somebody who will respect him. The bulk of the Russian people will be applauding all along the route, because they have had centuries of Imperial oppression, followed by six months of relative freedom and seventy years of the Gulag Archipelago. One can understand the relief at merely having a pumped-up ex-spy in charge who wants to make Russia great again.

<u>Luca</u> <u>Brasi</u> <u>and</u> <u>Why</u> <u>He</u> <u>is</u> <u>Important</u>

All persons who watched the movie "The Godfather" know who Luca Brasi is, even if they do not remember his name. He was the giant enforcer who asked a favor of Don Corleone at Sonny Corleone's wedding and was rewarded by Don Corleone's enemies when "The Turk" Virgil Sollozzo pinned his hand to a bar with a knife while a compatriot strangled him from behind. The suit later given to Sonny folded over a dead fish was Luca's suit. "Luca Brasi sleeps with the fishes."

In the movie everyone was afraid of Luca Brasi but it was never spelled out why. Francis Coppola tried to convey a natural brutishness adhering to a man, Lenny Montana, who had actually been a mafioso as well as a professional wrestler. It was not successful because of Montana's stage fright. In the book written by Mario Puzo, however, the characters are not merely afraid of Luca Brasi. They are terrified by him, especially the men. Even The Turk and his accomplices are terrified of him. This is why when they meet with him, they take no chances. Everyone has a supernatural fear of him. Their perceptions of him are phobic.

Why is this? This question, Puzo answers in the book. In his youth Brasi had an affair with an Irish prostitute who became pregnant.

Brasi wanted no part of a child born to an Irish woman. So he snatched the baby up, and took it to the basement, where he pitched it into the furnace fire. Even thinking about it is terrifying, and horrifying. To the typical Sicilian man, his children are gifts direct from God.

Terror and horror are not the same as fear, and they are not merely fear amplified. Brasi did not become more dangerous because he threw his baby into the furnace, but the horror of it puts terror in the heart. One shrank from facing him up, not because of fear, but on account of a phobic reaction to the inner terror.

This is the reason why some tyrannical leaders succeed wildly. Saddam Hussein struck terror in the Iraqi heart. The Iraqis knew he took pleasure in hurting them. The same with the Somozas in Nicaragua. This is why the Venezuelans only fear Nicolas Maduro, when Hugo Chavez terrified them. They knew he was loony tunes. Pinochet was a sadist. So was Ruhollah Khomeini. The first people he retained from the Shah were his infamously sadistic secret police.

This is why Luca Brasi is important. He was not the worst of people, but he was the worst of fathers, and an evil presence that panics the beating heart.

<u>Is</u> <u>Trumpism</u> <u>Chivalry's</u> <u>Revival</u> <u>or</u> <u>its</u> <u>Death</u> <u>Rattle?</u>

The presumptive reaction to the word "chivalry" is imagining a quaint set of customs in a fairy tale age long ago, when knights errant rescued damsels in distress, troubadours serenaded their sweethearts on moonlit nights, and courtly manners reigned supreme in a social life ruled by symbology, flags and pennants galore decorating the court. A noble, naïve people living a fantasy life that died a lovely romantic death on the golden brick road leading to the Renaissance.

In his excellent little 1925 book The Waning of the Middle Ages, Johan Huizinga makes the case that the dying breath of chivalry actually gave out in an atmosphere of dissipation, fear of the future, and unease about the general aims of European society. There had been certainty about chivalry and medieval life. Its highly codified and stratified sociology meant that everyone knew their places, status was known and honored, the Church was the reservoir of truth, everyone conformed to observed standards, and few secrets could be kept inside the village.

When the movement of trade, interest in science, and the wealth of aristocracy led to an interest in art, supplanting to a degree the demands of religion, and the rebirth of the great cities overwhelmed the interest in village life, the Renaissance was born. Cavalry warfare gave way to armed infantry and artillery. Seafaring trade dwarfed overland routes. The knight errant was no longer a useful occupation. Little by little, money encroached on status and property as the prime determinant of value.

Nevertheless, some of the core values of chivalry persisted in the idealistic side of European society: belief in the Church, honesty, valor, defense of the poor, humility, courtesy, fairness in commerce, honorable conduct, and regard for women. It has to be admitted that the last was a double-edged sword, since chivalry did not recognize women as equals, but as beautiful creatures to be protected. Valuable and cherished property, in other words.

The Trumpistas think that they are engaged in the long-sought rebirth of nobility, strength, and courage, and if they knew enough about it, they would imagine they are knights errant on a crusade to restore America. They certainly have the conformism well in hand, the notion that everybody must feel, be, and act the same. They certainly feel they are glorious. They certainly believe in symbols, not facts. Where, however, are the defense of the poor, the honesty, the fairness, humility, courtesy, honorable conduct in all things, and the rest of the chivalric ideals? Chivalry was not a style, a fashion statement, a sentiment.

It was a way of life.

NAKED CITY

What happened last night? The sky is so blue.
The naked city revels in its hue.
Where are the grime, the grit and the pallor?
The yellowed edges and the haze of gunfire
Wafting to the nose along the breezes
After a black night of desolation?
Burn, baby, burn in the glimmer of night,
The deadly sparkle of the urban light.

Gone, all gone the pain. The clouds are so white.
Blue deep blue as sky can be like sea blue.
The Cozumel channel never bluer,
The clouds white so white as a full moon
In black sky the whole universe seizes
In silence, stills the mind in awe full-blown.

The Real Iranian Revolution

It is a given in the West that Ruhollah Khomeini was a revolutionary. The pertinent question was and still is what kind of revolution was it, and what kind of man was he? It is fairly clear that the Carter Administration, who sent an envoy to him in a Paris suburb prior to the overthrow of the Shah, misread him completely. Did it come from mistaking him for a kindly old man, an Iranian patriot in robes, the image of an old prophet, Moses maybe?

The very picture of a reactionary throwback, Khomeini was anything but. He was known to the Iranian poor through years of radio broadcasts from Iraq, and later, from cassette tapes widely distributed in street markets. The middle class had hardly heard of him, and for the government, the military elite, or even the clerical establishment, he was a nobody. Only forty per cent of the population had any idea who he was. Part of the reason for this was the nature of Shi'i Islam itself.

Shi'i Islam was notable for being an orthopraxy, not an orthodoxy, as Sunni Islam is. If you paid your religious tax and observed all the proper devotions and practices, for the vast public this was the beginning and the end of religious obligations for the Shia. The believers were free to form their own opinions on any subjects, political or otherwise, that the clergy had not addressed directly. The status of the Grand Ayatollah was that of a theological leader, not a political one.

Ruhollah Khomeini did not qualify. He had little theological credibility, so his moves after returning to Iran were to solidify support, first among anti-Shah elite youth, and second, among the neighborhood leaders in Teheran. The first he got by promising to return to Constitutional law and install the vote, and the second, by encouraging Revolutionary Councils on the street to take the law into their own hands. Despite the contrary nature of these two models of society, his scheme succeeded. The next thing he did was to install the Shah's secret police as his own security force.

He did not return to the rule of law, he compromised the vote, and he let the Revolutionary Councils run amok for as long as it was useful to him. His notion of the people was that they were wards of the state, and his notion of the state was that it held all the rights, conferred by religion as he saw it. He flipped Shi'i Islam on its head, and he turned local leadership over to mullahs who had no training in, or aptitude for, governance and to Revolutionary Guards who took over the ad hoc Revolutionary Councils. Shi'i Islam became political from top to bottom.

In other words, he was the most radical leader in Shia history. There was nothing traditional about him. This was the main thing that threw the experts for a loop. It was not Khomeini against the Shah. It was Khomeini against centuries of tradition.

A LOS CUATRO VIENTOS HACE

La hediondez alcanza por todas partes.
No se puede desatender el olor. Los muertos
Caminan por las ruinas de ideas putrefactas.
En sus maletas traen los restos de sus parientes.
La carga estira los brazos suyos
Hasta que los dedos al polvo trazan el sendero
Hacía un sin fin de cosas malditas.
Una muñeca andrajosa duerme al fango
En lontananza. Los huesos de ella se proyectan
Por la ropa. Al paisaje entero los ladronzuelos
Ratean los bolsillos de los agonizantes.
Cierto que sí nadie no le importa.
El viento, el hedor, son naturales.
Lo natural está, lo bueno.
Una naturaleza, muerta.

<u>THE</u> <u>FOUR</u> <u>WINDS</u> <u>BLOW</u>

The stench stretches every which way.
The smell cannot be ignored. The dead
Walk through the ruins of putrefied ideas.
In their bags they carry the remains of their relatives.
The load stretches their arms
Until their fingers trace in the dust the path
Toward all manner of cursed things.
A ragged doll sleeps in the mud
In the distance. Her bones stick
Through her clothes. In the whole landscape
The petty thieves pick the pockets of the dying.
Certainly no one cares.
The wind, the stink, they are natural.
That which is natural is good.
A still life, death.

Some Quirks of the Civil War at the Outset

It is safe to say that the United States has never got over the Civil War, as recent events have made clear. It is even safer to say that its reasons and causes are as poorly understood today as they were when it happened.

It has generally been taught in the schools as a battle royal over good and evil. There is good reason for this, since there was a wrong and a right side to it in the plain and basic human terms of the abomination of slavery, but it is also a little simple-minded. It was an enormously complex social event.

In fact it was not really taken all that seriously in the very beginning. At the First Battle of Bull Run, spectators attended with box lunches to view the fighting, as if it were simply a blood sport.

The war could conceivably have ended at Shiloh, since a Union assault on the Confederate position was perfectly feasible, but the Union command staff sat on their heels. They did not surveill the Confederate forces. They failed even to cut a perimeter in the forest and man a blockade to forestall the eventual Confederate assault.

They could have taken Richmond at the outset and nullified the Confederate General Staff, and in the standard history fare of the Lincoln hagiography, the lackluster performance in Virginia is largely attributed to the timidity of George McLellan, commanding the Army of the Potomac. Accounts less attendant to the Lincoln hagiography have suggested that McLellan had promised to take Richmond in two weeks if Lincoln would just take off the handcuffs, but the President was terrified of McLellan's political ambitions.

Confederate troops were poorly supplied in every way, including basic victuals, low on meat and grain and constantly suffering fatigue. A cheap and easily transportable expedient was found in whiskey, which the metabolism will use for energy when glucose levels are low. The drawback was not always obvious, and many Confederate units were half-drunk half the time. (The role of whiskey in the post-War Westward expansion has never really been examined either.)

In the end it was a war of attrition, as Grant surmised after Shiloh, making him the first modern commander. If you have enough men and materiel, you can win a war through dogged pursuit. It does not replace tactical superiority but it makes up for many small mistakes.

<u>Who are the Taliban?</u>

It's high time to dispose of a couple of absurd notions about Afghanistan. One is general and the other is area-specific.

The general notion to discard is the idea that a foreign power can win a civil war. All a foreign power can do is take one side or the other, if there are clear sides to take, and aid and abet it. If that side wins, then the foreign power retires and takes its spoils how it can, either directly or indirectly. If the foreign power persists in thinking that it can win, then the conflict continues.

The specific notion is that Afghanistan is a failed state. It is not a failed state. It is a state that has been ruined by foreign powers, first by the Soviet Union, and second by the United States. From the late nineteen-twenties until the late nineteen-seventies Afghanistan had a stable if somewhat ineffectual government under a monarchy administered by a capable, educated, somewhat underpaid and understaffed civil service.

After the Soviet Union retired from the intervention, largely because their population grew sick and tired of seeing the body bags come home, Afghanistan was thrown into turmoil. The government had been destroyed, the civil service had all fled to the

West, where they had been educated, and over a million refugees ended up in Pakistan. Unemployed and broke, they saved their children by putting them in madrassas run by an Indian sect of far right Salafist Muslims, who would at least feed them. There these boys were indoctrinated in extremism rather than taught. They were taught how to fall into religious trances reciting their lessons over and over. These were the Taliban, a sort of bastardized plural form of "student."

During the consequent extreme de-stabilization of Afghan politics, amid constant internecine warfare, the United States cooked up the idea of returning the Afghan population by arming and assisting the Taliban, now young men. They were trained and led by the Pakistani secret service, the ISI, funded to the tune of hundreds of millions of dollars by the CIA. The promise made to the American government was that the Taliban would destroy the Afghan drug trade, source of most of the world's heroin. Because it was too lucrative, the Taliban did not do so, and then they became the solution that was worse than the problem.

The Taliban that is spoken about in the news today does not devolve from that Taliban. It is a reference to criminal tribal mobs that operate in Afghanistan from bases in Western Pakistan. They have their own agenda, which includes control of the lucrative drug trade, they are not unified, and it is easy for them to run protection rackets for a living. A war cannot be won there without a cultural revolution that, by definition, precludes ignorant outsiders like the United States.

O VANITY UNHINGED

You who have such tender vanities
A scratch bleeds for days, nay weeks on end,
Do plunder others' pain to satisfy
Delusions craftier than thinking will allow,
A cruelty greater than time can heal, were
The good flesh willing. Where intent is real
Remorse is false. And satisfaction
That creeps on itself and devours
Itself and lives in its own hot wet darkness
Unlimned, for it is the nameless unread
Unreadable.

(You know who you are.)

<u>The</u> <u>Pardon</u> <u>Power,</u> <u>What</u> <u>it</u> <u>is</u> <u>and</u> <u>is</u> <u>Not</u>

Let's go over this.

A pardon is a not a finding of innocence. It is not a finding of not guilty. It is not a finding of anything about a crime. It is a finding about punishment. It is a finding about punishment for a crime.

A pardon is not absolution for a crime. It does not absolve one for the finding of guilt. What it does is absolve one from the sentence for the crime. It is absolution for punishment. Joe Arpaio, for instance, will not be punished, but he can never try through appeal to reverse the guilty finding.

A pardon and guilt go together like the sky and the direction up. If there is no crime, there is no justification for a pardon. If a wrongful conviction is suspected, the legal remedy is not a pardon. In this case, the pardon is a practical remedy—a political act, not a jurisprudential one—that still does not produce a finding of innocence.

Even in the Nixon case, which was a general pre-emptive pardon for any and all events, and absolute in its extension, the feeling that crimes had been committed was both widespread among legal cognoscenti and particular in the understanding of Gerald Ford. When Ford went to Nixon to ask him to accept a pardon (and this was the way it happened, Ford going to Nixon), he carried with him a paper for Nixon to sign, admitting guilt. Nixon refused to admit guilt, and Ford pardoned him anyway after some negotiations. In effect, it was absolution from being tried for crime, although one legal theory held that he could still be compelled to give testimony to Congress for his crimes, and Special Counsel Leon Jaworski gave an opinion later that the evidence for indictments was overwhelming.

The Department of Justice protocol for a pardon proffer is the acknowledgment of guilt on the part of the pardoned. A pardon must be accepted as well as given, and one of the conditions is a finding of guilt. Another condition is a waiver of the Fifth Amendment right to avoid self-incrimination in a hearing before the Congress or in testimony before a court concerning crimes by other persons.

However, the idea that a federal pardon does not preclude trial in state criminal courts has not been tested. After this mess with Donald Trump, who knows how many precedents will be established, for good or for ill.

<u>A</u> <u>New</u> <u>Wrinkle</u> <u>On</u> <u>the</u> <u>Pardon</u>

This is a new wrinkle on the subject. It was brought up in a news interview of a legal historian at Fordham named Jed Shugerman.

This is a bit complicated although it is not long. If I understand it correctly it is a theory that a pre-emptive pardon does not protect the pardonee from every future jeopardy. A blanket pardon would cover all criminal charges regardless of time frame. Would it guarantee, however, the meaning of the legal term "to be held harmless" in each and every case? What about an act for which the pardonee was not responsible?

For instance, if the pardonee were to perjure himself in the future about an act <u>that</u> <u>occurred</u> <u>before</u> <u>the</u> <u>pardon</u> <u>was</u> <u>made</u>, would the perjury be excluded from the pardon? If it would be excluded, as Mr.Shugarman argued, the pardonee would no longer have the protection of the Fifth Amendment after being charged with the perjury. Accepting the pardon would have voided his right to plead the Fifth. Accordingly, testimony about the perjury could be compelled under the threat of further charges, and this would naturally include testimony about the original act, the subject of the perjury.

It sounds arcane, and something that law students would love to debate in moot court, but you never know. Its utility in a legal proceeding might be tested on the ground.

SEPTEMBER..................

Deconstruction of the Administrative State

The first time I heard this phrase, two words came to mind: Jacques Derrida. I know I was not alone, but I could not be among the many. This brought up the second thought: At last we have politicians who have heard of writers other than Ayn Rand. Then came the third thought: Good grief! Now that we have politicians who have heard of Jacques Derrida, therefore deconstructivism will be taken seriously. Studying decconstructivism seriously means that understanding a paragraph takes days.

Anarchists we have always had. Jefferson was a sort of mild anarchist. And McKinley was the kind of guy who wanted to see government get out of the way of business. To get to a politician who wanted actually to downsize government programmatically, another phrase for deconstruction of the administrative state, we have to fast-forward to Jimmy Carter. Then along came Reagan with the idea that the federal government was the main problem and later Bill Clinton, whose idea was to cut the federal workforce substantially, and let the budget wither.

After two successive administrations that have expended enormous amounts of money, some of it off-budget, pursuing foreign adventures of dubious merit, now we have an administration who wants to tear it all down. Its mavens want to eliminate foreign entanglements, keep foreigners out, and pay down social programs. One of their methods is simply to de-fund anything they disfavor, a probable violation of a forty year old federal statute. I.e., probably a crime, not that it will be prosecuted.

What is the general aim and how is it supposed to be put in place? These two questions have actually not been answered. Why is this? Is it that they are incapable of producing a viable mission statement, or is the intellectual confusion so great that they are incapable of analyzing the problem. "Make American Great Again" is not a program. Clinton said it, and Reagan before him. Politicians as disparate as Clinton, Reagan, and Trump saying the same thing means by definition that the statement itself has no intrinsic meaning. It is simply a slogan to attract attention. Everybody prefers being great to being puny. The question is how? By asserting personal power over shared values?

It is no secret that federal agencies are being directed to defeat the laws that are their charters. EPA, HUD, Education, HHS, State, etc. are all working to kill their own programs. What could it be that makes these efforts great? How could they help people? Is the fundamental Trump program to redevelop the backward areas of the economy? Is it to make investments safe for the most forward areas? To effect a monoculture? If you deconstruct the administrative state, how do you construe the programs you want? With what do you administer them?

<u>Bannon</u> <u>and</u> <u>the</u> <u>Truth</u>

"The truth is not contingent on recognition." I wish I could remember who said this. I know that I said it, but I believe I lifted it from some venerable old philosopher somewhere sometime. Steal if you can, I always say.

Like millions of others I heard Steve Bannon telling Charlie Rose that the firing of Jim Comey was the worst mistake made in modern political history. Of course, this does turn on the definition of "modern," but I think we can safely assume that it means after World War II.

The only problem then is what "worst" means. From Eisenhower to Clinton nearly every President committed some egregious political error. George W. lied in order to acquire the invasion of Iraq next to his name. Nixon fired Archibald Cox. Through eleven Presidents, the list of errors is not exactly a short one.

We should not be too surprised at Bannon's grasp of the moment, however. He himself claims to be a bombastic type, and this may be due to his misunderstanding of the word "bombast." It means more than exaggeration or a loud tone. More or less, it means spouting off platitudes and lies vigorously with hearty arm-waving.

I mean, some of his political and historical opinions are preposterous and ill-founded without necessarily being bombastic. The idea that the American economy was originally founded by Americans for Americans has a good sound to it, but not the ring of truth. For the first hundred years anybody could get in the United States. Immigrant controls was a phrase *non sequitur.*

Take the idea that the American economy failed to grow unless the government let business alone. In truth, the budding industrial economy was developed by the Whigs doing the exact opposite, promoting business. Later, the "let-alone" slogan was perverted to connote, Let the people alone to fend for themselves.

The notion that globalism is a recent economic vision of the Bushes and Clintons is pure unbaked fiction, wet dough. Globalism goes back to the 1880's when the robber barons started to realize that Manifest Destiny did not create a large enough market. American industry needed to branch out into economic colonialism, force open the doors to foreign markets, the Open Door Policy.

Nevertheless, we should be charitable criticizing the judgment of a guy who banks on splitting apart his own political party to get what he wants. He should go for it.

<u>Bannon</u> the <u>Liar</u>

Steve Bannon is a liar. This does not mean that he spends his time mouthing off febrile untruths. The disconnect between him and the patent truth is both more mysterious and more subterranean.

One, he is an ignorant man whose self-validated theories inform his feeble grasp of society and history. Delusional, in other words, without being clinically ill. The difference is that his mythology is custom-made rather than handed down whole, as is the case with most Americans. Therefore the critical analysis of it takes more work and imagination than it may be worth.

Two, he is a manipulator. He would simply be another opinion-monger like Rush Limbaugh and Alex Jones if it were not for the incipient megalomania, the closet self-absorption. He is the Iago to Trump's Othello, except that the jealousy is not configured on romance and the central mystery does not concern a trivial item like a scarf. Otherwise, the Trump saga and Othello present the same bombast and intrigue and the same baffling core to the narrative. Nobody knows exactly what anyone else wants, and the tragic end seems senseless.

Of course, we have not reached the end of the story. Nor will we ever be clear about the essence of Bannon's dissimulation. More probably than not, we will never see this for what it is, because it is likely that Bannon himself does not know it for what it is. The evidence that he is an actor talented enough to shuck and jive a global flock of rubes simply does not look to be there. That he seems sincere about his beliefs is both the best and the worst thing about him. This is not the same as guessing that he is a nice guy underneath the bluster, a highly unlikely scenario.

People who believe in the soundness of their own fairy tales are hard to knock off their seats. They know the content better than anyone else, and they are more motivated to defend themselves than others are to attack them.

However, there is another big lie to Bannon. This revolves around the so-called populism. When you boil this down in the Bannon kitchen, it looks like the genuine All-Mystic Full-Flavored white male machismo stew. This is the populism of the twenty-five per cent. If plenty of the white women did not relish this arcane high-protein diet, it would be the populism of the twelve point five per cent.

Not exactly a promising start for the revolution to a brave new world.

<u>Trump's U. N. Speech, September 19, 2017.</u>

If it were an IT coming-of-age script, the U. N. speech yesterday would be about a precocious thirteen year old smart-ass writing a payback speech to be delivered by his twelve year old bully buddy to scare all the adults in the school. The venue is a school merit function held in the auditorium, but instead of awards, the boy announces that the school has been booby-trapped. If the adults refuse to go along with a series of insane demands, the digital buttons will be pushed one by one.

Only it is not a pre-teen disaster movie, the irrational text has instead been written by a goony assistant acting out multiple personality disorders, and the speech is given by an American President who could not think his way out of a mixed metaphor. The audience sits open-mouthed throughout. The speaker only delivers one rigorous applause line, and that a cynical and disingenuous encomium to women's rights. He calls the United Nations "they," not "we."

He walked out of the building saying that he believed the speech went well, while the over-under line for most of the commentators was that it was incoherent bluster unworthy of the Presidential office. Nonetheless, Trump's friends in Congress called it bold, and even the Democrats tried to find some solace in it, exactly what you would expect of the most cowardly Congress in history. Rex Tillerson, the worst Secretary of State in history, called it an effective way to unite the world, and John Negroponte, the kindly butcher of El Salvador and Guatemala under Reagan, called it a fairly good review of critical issues.

Accordingly, Trump had waxed pseudo-religious, speaking of good and evil, talking about countries going to Hell without saying who or why. He lamented the "wicked" states. He exhorted the good nations to get together in fighting evil. He assumed that he was among the righteous and explained that he takes it upon himself to "totally destroy North Korea" if he has to prove his essential holiness.

To enlighten the U. N., a body designed to promote peace in the world and to explore common aims, he described a world order in which cooperation is only a smart tactic. Sovereignty is the key attribute. It is the Ayn Rand plan of action, a scheme of international relations that might be called "every dog buries its own bone." It might also be named the Putin model of diplomacy.

Because it is a title system geared to heavyweights, it will not go very far on the world stage. Of course the heavyweights would want all the championship belts if they could get them. It would be a bully's paradise.

Letter To an Old Friend Who Will Not be Named

You think that the hood rats, the warwhoops, and the spicks ought to step 'n fetchit, get on with it, and clam up. Start acting like all the good little palefaces who never make waves.

You're not a conservative. George Will and Clarence Thomas are conservatives. What you are is a narrow-minded conformist with a mean streak and an axe to grind. An authoritarian. You believe you belong to a superior culture without understanding what a culture is or how it works.

And I'm not a liberal. I'm much worse than that. I'm a hard-nosed two-fisted gun-loving free-thinking radical who hates the one-size-fits-all theory of sociology more than you do because it's stupid and it saps the human spirit. I'd save you from a burning building but I wouldn't walk across the street to explain anything to you. I wouldn't waste my time.

OCTOBER……………..

The Memory of Charles Whitman

In searching for a reason why the mad mass murder act by Stephen Paddock in Las Vegas—as if there could be anything about reason in it—several commentators have dredged up the name of Charles Whitman. Charles Whitman was the University of Texas Tower sniper. He killed several people in 1966. The reason why people bring up Charles Whitman is that subsequently, an autopsy found that he had a brain tumor, and the common rumor is that the brain tumor caused the disability that turned him into a killer.

It is not uncommon for people to look for reasons why heinous crimes are committed. It has been found that many serial killers have neurological deficits in the frontal lobe. It has been found that many murderers have suffered brain injuries, they were sexually abused as children, have a history of juvenile crime, and are epileptic. These are not reasons they are killers, however. If the conditions are turned around and we examine people with neurological deficits in the frontal lobe, other brain injuries, been sexually abused, committed juvenile crime, and suffer from epilepsy, we do not find that they are all killers.

So, there is something else that makes them killers and something normal that prevented them for some time from becoming killers, and that is the normal functioning of the frontal lobes, which rule the faculties of judgment. People who know not to kill do not suddenly become killers because they have a brain injury or they have suffered some setback or rejected in love or made angry by being thwarted in some ambition. This desire to kill cannot be normalized by finding a reason to do it, some sense in it. The senseless does not have sense in it.

This brings us back to Charles Whitman. There is a common misunderstanding as to who Charles Whitman was. He was not a normal person who suddenly became a killer on account of a brain tumor.

I am guessing—a guess, a hunch—that in Stephen Paddock there was not some benign stillness inside that was thrown off the track somehow and turned bad. I am also guessing that someone knew this. It was not the number and type of guns he owned. It was that he carried so many with him. The normal person does not carry twenty-some guns to his hotel room to go gambling. If he had forty-some guns, why did he leave some at home? Very little about this makes sense. It was certainly planned, but the existence of planning is not contingent on good sense.

<u>Trump's</u> <u>Secret</u> <u>Goal</u>

In the foothills of the Blue Ridge mountains west of Charlottesville VA, and maybe elsewhere in the South, white men of a certain political and social bent used to play an obscure game. It was a game played on the country roads in and between the small towns, and it may still be played. Not all white men played this game, but notably the ones afflicted with a certain skin color deformity of the neck.

This game was not really a game. It was a sort of trick practiced on members of the human race disliked by these funny rash-necked white men. In a word it was a prank. It was not a benign sort of prank. It was more like the opposite of benign. It was more on the order of a crime, almost certainly a felony. One had to have a car in order to do it and the spare time it took to find an available opponent.

The name of this game was "brooming ni**ers." A group of men—it took at least two—rode around the small towns and the country lanes looking for African-Americans walking the road shoulder on the right side. They had to be walking with traffic instead of the recommended practice of facing it.

Playing the game required a broom, hence the name of the game. Only the mounted players got one. The opponent on foot played without an implement. When the players in the car found a suitable opponent, they stuck the broom out the window to strike him or her with. This move produced a win. The reward for the winners was to drive away laughing. The person walking could only lose.

This is the game that Donald Trump would like to play with Barack Obama, if he knew about it and could have the opportunity. He will not have the opportunity, so he must make the psychological transference of wrecking Obama's legacy. It is his secret goal, an open secret, to broom Obama.

<u>General Kelly's Apologia Yesterday</u>

While it appears that Chief of Staff Kelly's preferred encomium to fallen military loved ones—he knew what he was in for— has the same substance as President Trump's phone call to LaDavid Johnson's widow, there are certain tenable differences. The first one is that Kelly has relevant military experience to draw on. The second is the narrative sequence of statements, Trump's remarks seeming to make it sound like death was the eventuality bargained for and sorrow simply the upshot. A punctured balloon.

In Mr. Kelly's opinion of a proper condolence, like that received for his own son, the first thing to note was that his son was a military son, and the second that he understood the values of his family. It should also be noted that Kelly received his consolation from a consigned peer, his casualty officer. Speaking to a peer officer is not the same way one would talk to an aggrieved widow, who is not a military veteran. She is responding to an irrepressible loss in her personal life, first and foremost.

The whole tone and temper of Kelly's remarks are more quietist than Trump's declamation, especially if we take into account the President's petulant reaction to the charge of being boneheaded. His pushback was not only angry. It was also hostile, filled with a veiled threat of retaliation. A sincere person who had got it wrong unintentionally in the first place would normally be eager to make it right in the aftermath. Trump's doubling down, however, made it seem entirely likely that he was incapable of the tender mercy required up front.

Of course, no one was surprised that Trump might have got it wrong. After all, this is the same man who responded to the murder of an innocent by a white supremacist at a combined neo-Nazi/KKK-sympathizer rally by claiming that there were bad people on both sides, and good ones siding with the suspect.

Speaking of tone-deafness, some of us might spot a little scuffmark on Kelly's shoes. During his remarks, he noted that the military do not dislike the general public. As a matter of fact, he said, those in uniform feel sorry for them for not having had the military experience—the esprit de corps and the personal fulfillment. Taken by itself, this sounds like the tired old moral one-up of the military writ, one of the things that has done so much to divide American society since the Cold War started.

Like everything else, it all depends on how the argument is laid out and in what tone of voice. If it was San Diego in the late sixties, the sociology was all too often Marines looking for hippies to beat up. The Marines were clearly one up at that. Nonetheless, undoubtedly Kelly would disfavor knuckle-dusting to settle the moral philosophy issue. It is not so clear that Trump would.

The <u>Empty</u> <u>Barrel</u> <u>Trope</u>

Let's take a look at the phrase "empty barrel", what it means, what it excepts, and whom it designates. The admonition "an empty barrel makes the most noise" is generally addressed to people whom you consider your inferior, such as students by their teacher. According to people who went to Catholic schools, it was a favorite of the nuns to stifle the hijinks of the attention-disabled.

You don't generally hear adults calling other adults "empty barrels," no matter what the venue is. Calling someone else an "empty barrel" in a bar argument is likely to incite violence, if it is not so unusual that it occasions a shrug of the shoulders and a quizzical, "What the hey did he say?" In a union hall, it would be an invitation to a Mexican standoff, where nothing is gained and everybody loses.

So, therefore, when Chief of Staff John Kelly called Congresswoman Frederica Wilson an "empty barrel," the first signal he made was "I'm superior" and the second was "you're not doing anything but making noise." Under the circumstances, it would be easy to imply that the assumed superiority had a racial element. [After all, none of the white soldiers' families were subjected to any such degradation, so far as we know.] Kelly was also telling her that she had nothing to say—her barrel was empty—implying that his own barrel was full. How else could he know? It was not a conditional charge, making the case that she was ignorant on a particular issue. He actually raised it in a recount of a separate and unrelated encounter; in so doing he demeaned her character and intelligence.

Kelly has claimed that he was "stunned" by hearing Congresswoman Wilson's remarks at the dedication of an FBI building in Miami in 2015, because it proved "how empty her barrel was." In fact, most of her speech reflected why the FBI building was named for two Special Agents who were slain in the line of duty. She then asked the Special Agents in attendance to stand that they could be recognized.

Two days ago John Kelly disrespected Frederica Wilson, not professionally, but personally. You could see his jaw quiver when he called her simply "the Congresswoman" without appending her name. Apparently he could not bring himself to say her name. He knew it. He made it clear he knew who she was.

Yesterday Sarah Huckabee Sanders was sent out to defend his statements, and the upshot of this was the remarkable charge that the press had no business questioning a Four Star General. Since when? This was "stunning." It looked like proof that Donald Trump was indeed the right person for Kelly to be working for.

The Center of It All

Ideology is the enemy of sense. Everything practical and feasible is provisional. Provided this, do that. Given that, do this.

Everything sustainable in life happens in the middle. The likely thing is not the one sitting at the boundary. The center is where the action is. The center is where the gravity is, and gravity is serious business.

Of course, knowing where the center is means taking the measure of all things. Politically, throughout the inventions of the modern industrial state, the great pendules of society have been the left and the right, the force of the people and the force of tradition. This no longer obtains. The battle now is the struggle between those who want to make rules and those who want to make money. This is the clash between fear and greed.

The so-called liberals believe that one size fits all, and this is patent nonsense. All endeavor is conditioned by circumstance. Neglecting this leads to the familiar quandary of the square peg and the round hole. The so-called conservatives are even worse. They believe that there are no sizes, and this leads to the condition of those who get there first, wherever it is, get the most. The prize goes to the ambitious. Blind ambition is a virtue.

Those who believe in the center have been taught that they must take a choice. Not taking a choice is identified with being namby-pamby, wishy-washy, muddled by compromise. The concept of a two-fisted hard-nosed no-holds-barred centrist is tantamount to madness. If it were in the arena, it would be laughed out. Instead of a melee in the middle of the square, where the way to do things has to be worked out, what we have is a tug of war, where clearly defined teams reach a Mexican standoff. This futile standstill lasts until one side can recruit enough members of the other to defect and pull the other out the door. There they can be locked out.

This results in the tyranny of the fifty-one per cent. No compromise, no agreement, only acquiescence or defeat. Triumph and grievance. Power and vengeance. No change can be reached but reversal.

The alternative demands a change of heart. It requires working out disagreements rather than fighting over them. It takes giving up the damn fool search for the ideal solution. The perfect solution is an ideological myth. The adequate solution is the best one can do, and the job is never done. Life happens in the middle.

Small-town Nostalgia

It is wonderful to think back on an age a half century ago, more or less, when houses went unlocked, kids played untended between school's last bell and dinner time, and happiness seemed a hope within easy reach. Nostalgia casts a rosy glow on the wistful mists of memory.

It is easy to forget that this was the period when the Cold War cast a global pall of fear, the Soviet Union put long-range missiles on Cuba, and military reservists were called on to defend Berlin. It is easy to forget that some hard-line conservatives applauded John Kennedy's assassination. Where I grew up, a high school employee was heard to say, "It's about time," and he was not disciplined.

The narrow-mindedness is easy to forget, as well as the pervasive social conformism. It was a time when some Oregon high school students were arrested and charged with crime for running a hammer-and-sickle flag up the school pole as a prank. Block monitors were hired by some city governments to report on their neighbors' "suspicious" activities, just as they did in Russia and Cuba. It was a time when Presidents of Draft Boards angrily called you a "pinko" to your face if you questioned the wisdom of the Vietnam adventure.

Often the local courts pursued different policies for defendants from good families and defendants who came from the wrong side of the tracks, the "Pettyvilles" and the "South Sides" and the "Bottoms." People were charged with property crimes for where they lived and what their reputations were, not what they did.

Numerous men suffered from PTSD on account of the Korean War and World War II. Many drank heavily. Drunken fistfighting was common in the streets by the bars. The fighting ethos spilled out to the schools, where bullies ruled playgrounds unchecked. Child-beating was commonplace, and not just simple spankings.

The schools themselves were ruled by humorless principals who kept paddles in their offices. The teaching of discipline was often considered the highest aim of education. Corporal punishment was rarely challenged by parents.

Racism, both overt and covert, went uncorrected. Jews changed their names to operate under the radar. If you sat out in your yard of a warm summer night and watched the stars, you were thought suspicious. It was a wonderful time when it was wonderful, but it was also an awful time if you looked at it close.

<u>The</u> <u>White</u> <u>Liberal's</u> <u>Biggest</u> <u>Fear</u>

To be the only white person at a black wedding.

There you find out that big-hat ladies are commonplace. Not just commonplace, but expected. The ceremony will be noisy with the Praise-be's, the Yes-Lords, and the Amens. Everybody will dance, including the kids and the octogenarians, at the reception, and more food will be piled on your plate than you can possibly eat. People will talk loud and play the dozens at high volume as the drink takes hold, the women and the men both. The throwing of the garter is a big deal and captures everybody's attention. You will be made welcome, and you will still not know how to act. You won't know that natural is best.

Natural is best. This is the thing that has been bothering me about a certain liberal response lately to Congresswoman Frederica Wilson. Some people who admitted that she had a point in the latest Trumpish kerfuffle found her tacky, or embarrassing, or something. I'm not sure whether it was the loud hats, the loud clothing, the loud voice, or the loud confidence. All this may seem outlandish to the garden variety white liberal, but it is a cultural staple of the black experience.

The white liberals of two generations ago never imagined that black people, once accepted, would be who they were. They had in mind that black people would learn how to be white. They would give up their playing the dozens, their styling while they walk, their big hats, their loud conversations, the street theatre of their culture. And the white liberals have never got used to it, nor their children and grandchildren.

It is easy to point out that this is racist but hard to prove, since it is always covert and usually unconscious. Some white people's complaints about Michelle Obama's bare arms deflect the racism by calling attention to First Lady fashion norms, but no one has yet complained about Melania Trump's bare arms. They have made fun of Frederica Wilson's goofy hats, but everyone gave a pass to Kellyanne Conway's grotesquely hilarious nutcracker hat, and outfit, at the inaugural.

If you hint that someone is a covert racist, he or she is almost always mightily offended and accuses you of making a mountain out of a molehill. The how-dare-you routine is as predicative as it is predictable, a sure sign that white superiority —in contrast to white supremacy—is alive and well. It is nearly as much behavioral conformism as it is racial ignorance, but it is funny not ha-ha how often it shows its face in a racial format.

Killing the Moderates

The second thing that every successful revolution accomplishes is killing the moderates. The revolutionaries can tolerate the opposition because none of its followers will convert to the their world-view. They cannot tolerate the moderates because they are close enough to them to tempt their less ideological members, no matter what the ideology is.

After the Bolshevik revolution in Russia, Lenin first took over the banks and railroads. Second he destroyed all the socialists and all the movements toward local power, the local communes and all attempts at local organization, such as the Kronstadt Rebellion. Then he continued fighting the White Army.

Even revolutionaries who do not succeed follow the same model. In the same manner, Stalin took over leadership of the German Communist Party and directed them to destroy all the Socialist parties rather than fight the Nazis. At the time there was virtual civil war in the streets of the industrial north over control of German industry. Within a short time, the Nazi Party took over the parliament, building and all, and bullied the center-left coalition into voting for the Enabling Laws that gave them legal power to enact their program.

When the people of Nicaragua, led by the business community and organized by the Sandinistas, overthrew the Somoza family tyranny, the next thing that happened was that the Sandinistas drove out the moderates and took over the government. They had a specific socialist ideology and a program how to work it out. They had a well-prepared method. A few years after taking control of the country and installing elections, their main leader changed his career to wholesale used car sales. After returning to run for the Presidential office, he drove the moderates out again to put in place a tyrannical right wing form of government.

We are going through the same thing right now in this country. Donald Trump is the titular head of the administration, and he is trying to rid the government of moderates. The general aim seems to be installing a third-world style kleptocracy, no matter what his claqueurs like Steve Bannon and Stephen Miller want to call it. Economic nationalism or America First, the aim is philosophical fascism, top-down control of the state and its economy to produce wealth for the people running the government. The following part of the method, the third stage, is to hold the economy hostage to kleptocratic corruption, especially in banking, high-end real estate, and energy. The fact that the people who control banking, real estate, and energy now may object to the program does not seem to stop the Trumpistas from trying.

THE WRIT

I toiled in darkness, lingered in the shade
And raised my compass high above the sun
To see which way the north is true true north
Among the stars that twinkle in the black
Debacle where the Prince of Darkness makes
His bed his bed the hooves crash through the floor
Where floor is not the solid place where beds
Can rest the legs not tottering. The yawn.

The broom makes scratching sounds between the dust
And listless moaning of the chambermaids
Who dust the shelves with clean silk panties worn
By amateur transvestites once upon
A time in future fantasies. The scream
The carping started up with serious
Intent. The Prince of Darkness dithered. Yawn.
He could not wake awake he could not sleep.

The spot the not the bard's lament the out
That will not get the damned. And when the leaves
Upon the ground have all but turned the brown

That worms will one day turn to mud and up
The roots until the tree grows tall until
The autumn grows the sunset red and all
The light descends below the earth. The Prince
Of Darkness knows the way. He saw the writ.

Is Business Rational or Not?

Over the last few weeks, the news reporters, commentators, and anchors have been re-examining the business angle of the Trump Presidency, both in terms of the question how Trump could have succeeded in business without being rational and how business people could support him if he were not rational like them. The underlying assumption is that success in business is contingent on rationality.

Rather than looking at this in panoramic view or from the outside looking in, I want to tell you about my experience working for other people, and what I have seen of others working for other people. Having worked for several real estate development companies, both on staff and contracting, I can tell you that real estate companies are all over the map on the rational scale. They're always better on the buildings and the systems than they are on personnel management.

This brings me to the construction companies themselves. The larger they are, the better organized because building have to work right, and the accountants are sitting on their backs besides. This is not true among the sub-contractors. The subset of those companies has managers, and owners, that are described on every page of the diagnostic manual of psychiatry. Many of them do very well on the work itself and lack expertise on people skills and time management.

People generally have the idea that small retail businesses, particularly premium niche businesses like high-end alcohol and tobacco, must be run by rational actors because of product knowledge and the demands of upkeep. Nothing could be further from the truth. The principal skills that most of the owners have are a relative with money and the desperation that comes from the inability to get and keep a decent job. If I had time to tell you, I guarantee that most of you would be astonished at what infirmities of judgment they manage to survive.

Some of them are flat-out clinically ill upstairs and need medication, but they are usually high-performing, and they manage to skid through both angry fits with customers and overdone delirium too. Some of them run their business as if it were a love affair, complete with the whole emotional labyrinth. My dad knew his business backward and forward, but he was a gambler, and that was definitely irrational.

I have run businesses for other people, and there as often as not, you will make the owner angry if you do things better. Improvements that you develop in the system are likely to be turned down, especially if they show him or her up. The myth of the rational business person is just that, not a falsehood, but a myth.

[A successful businessman friend gave the answer as 50-50.]

Trump's Condition and the Psychiatrists Not Needed

Clearly, there is something wrong with Donald J. Trump, and no psychiatrist is needed to tell us what it is, what the proper diagnostic name for it is. We can see for ourselves the visible and palpable narcissism, a condition that has been recognized since classical Greece. Aligned with it is megalomania, a "greatness unrecognized" and self-pity from lamenting the lack of recognition. The mistaken monomanic compulsion to consider one's self in control of all things, when one is clearly not, invokes the Dunning-Kruger Effect, an incompetent person's inability to recognize his own incompetence. The Dunning-Kruger Effect has a corollary, the inability of the competent to recognize that the incompetent do not self-correct. Incompetence is a paroxysmal condition: whatever scheme the incompetent devises for correction makes the symptoms worse. In politics this belies the familiar, and ultimately melancholy, hope that the sufferer will learn on the job. No, this hope will be trampled underfoot.

Then there are the other symptoms. The juvenile lexicon, the simplified, disjointed syntax and the repetitions. The malapropisms: "the furniture of the youth, that is, the future." The non sequiturs: "Of course I'm civil. I went to an Ivy League college." Some unusual physical symptoms that everyone but those familiar with patients in mental institutions will miss. And others that we might infer from reports of his behavior in the White House residence, such as waking up angry and susceptible to delusions, a syndrome of mental disorder that some of us are familiar with in our own homes and know it requires medication.

Aside from these, we have seen the lying, the intentional verbal cruelty, the lability—i.e., the emotional unpredictability and responses well out of proportion to the stimulus, the inability to forget a grievance or recognize one's own mistakes, and other personal character defects that the psychiatrists have no cure for and disregard diagnostically. The same goes for the lack of empathy that they do have a name for and a description of, but no hint of a cure.

On the mean streets the technical psychiatric term for the disorder that Trump displays is bullshitting. It is also true that on the street bullshitting is an art form. For the art form the bullshitter has to maintain the craft of it and refrain from bullshitting the wrong people. Bullshitting the wrong people gets you hurt, and the bullshitter who has it as a compulsion invariably gets hurt sooner or later. It helps the artful bullshitter to be inventive and interesting as well as careful. If people like you, it goes a long way toward keeping the soles of your shoes underneath your feet. If you are not liked, it is a good idea to steer away from bullshitting altogether.

IN THE WIND THE DAYS FLY BY

All the feckless renegades knew the place.
The dusty river flowed past. The reckless
Bikers parked just up the street. Countless birds
Roosted in the willows on windless days
When cloudless skies ruled the blue horizons.

The road was dirt. The beer was cheap. The talk
Was empty, subject known to one and all,
The ease of solitude and dryness spent
Wondering when the rains would come and cows
Could find their feed without the rancher's help.

The women were bored. They had work to do
But work was not what they wanted. The wait
Discarded all the reasons. In the sack
With the spuds the patience went uncooked. Time
Lay tired on the counting. No use for it.

THE GLORY AND THE SHAME

"The glory and shame of the universe,"
Said Blaise Pascal. Blaise Cendrars said the same,
Although the same was awfully different.

I picked the right book to read off the shelf,
And then I threw it away in the trash.
The garbage is the place for it, the bin
Where Pirandello put his last copy
Of Beckett's "Endgame." Robert Walser did.

How many times will I think that Hitler
Was that scrawny kid in the back, his chair legs
Scratching, jumping up and down in his seat,
Alert to any hint that he was seen
By any eye aimed outside the window
Where later he would hold court yammering
All the damn fool ideas he could muster
And how all we had to was shut him up,
A dirty sock duct-taped inside his mouth?

"I am a member of the profession,"
Said John Carradine, showing off his voice.
And voice it was to show off too, a voice
Of glory and a shame it was not more,
The voice within that gives the tone of truth,
The universe and all that is and not.

NOVEMBER.....................

Who Was Eisenhower Really?

During the waning years of the Reagan Administration especially, at the height of Eisenhower's rehabilitation by liberals, you hardly heard his name without mention of his warning made about the military-industrial complex at the end of his political career. This has been taken to mean that he was prescient about the power signature of the federal government, the unnatural love affair, the ménage à trois of the military, the executive branch, and defense industries. Without this perversion of power, we would not have the crowing about a Pax Americana during the second Bush administration by old-guard liberals turned globalist conservatives, the neo-cons, or the concomitant encroachment on the State Department by military diplomatic missions both at home and overseas.

Ingenuously, it is simply assumed that Eisenhower had become opposed to a growing advance of the military into domestic politics through expanding the defense department's economic power and procurement capacity. This assessment of his departing speech is both too simple and too general.

Eisenhower came into office determined to see not only civilian leadership of the military restored after World War II and the

Korean War, but also to subordinate the military to the domestic economy. The Cold War would have an economic mission supported by the threat of massive sudden retaliation. Under this defense theory, the Air Force increased in importance, but the executive supervision of the military as a whole had become a cumbersome formal system that failed to control inter-service fighting over budgetary appropriations.

When Kennedy won the election, change was inevitable. Kennedy had no use for Eisenhower's defense policies or his construction of defense administration. He saw the older generation of military leaders as stuffy and inflexible, and he wanted an adaptable defense system. He had a free-wheeling manner of decision-making, an informal style of personnel management, and he wished to have a direct chain of command without rigid controls. He made these things known before inauguration, and he started making changes in top-ranking military personnel as well as the operational configuration of the military and security agencies.

Eisenhower did not trust Kennedy. He thought the warm, charming, witty Democrat was too inexperienced to deal with the military, too arrogant to learn how, too eager to make uninformed decisions, not wary enough of the defense industries' motives, and too impressed by self-absorbed intellectuals. When he made his speech, first of all he was talking to Kennedy.

Shakespeare in History

Now let's look at what you thought you saw when you read what I was saying. I did not say that Shakespeare was the sole or the first Elizabethan playwright or scholar to defy the providential view of the time. I did not say that he always represented this viewpoint. I did say that his work was "riven through" with the skepticism about providence.

I did not make any representation about the percentages of other Elizabethan playwright who shared or rejected his view. I did say that Shakespeare was the pinnacle of the field in that era, and I did say that many of his colleagues wrote entertainments. (In fact, there was a good deal of plagiarism in the era and chains of derivative story lines. The Hamlet is the obvious one.)

Obviously if one were to write serious historical drama, even if the history were not particularly accurate, one would attempt to portray important ideas integral to the narrative, such as the divine right of kings. However, if you take the story of Richard III that you cite, the big lesson that can be derived from the plot denouement is this: the conceit of the divine right of kings led Richard to defeat, death, and dishonor. He was defeated by men, he had put himself in jeopardy, and God did not save him.

(Personally, I have a particular reason to take a skeptical view of the Shakespeare scholars. For five hundred years they were unable to decipher what he meant by the hawk and handsaw reference. It is understandable that men without a callus on their hands might miss the definition, but not when it is perfectly obvious to a builder, or anybody who watched building being done, or certainly to a builder in Shakespeare's time and for centuries afterward. A "hawk" is the metal or wood plaque, held horizontally from a centered vertical post underneath it, that plasterers use to hold their mud while they are working it. Someone who doesn't know a hawk from a handsaw, therefore, is someone who doesn't know his asshole from his elbow. It has nothing to do with birds. In five hundred years one would think that there would be at least one scholar to cop to this.)

Otherwise, I don't object to anything you said. Harold Bloom might, or might have. I don't know. The providential view of history was the order of day in Stratford-on-Avon, a medieval-remnant town, and it is fairly remarkable that young William was not imbued with it. This is part of the wonder of Shakespeare's career.

<u>Who</u> <u>John</u> <u>Kennedy</u> <u>Was</u>

No one has to tell me who John F. Kennedy was. He was the bright shining light of the nineteen-sixties. Richard M. Nixon was the galactic black hole.

Kennedy gave millions of American teenagers hope for the future. He told them that they were important, and that the best thing they could do to show it was to love their country and do what they could to help it. His appeal was not political. It was personal, and it was patriotic. Sure, he had political reasons to say so, but it was not cynical.

In the Sixties, the cynicism came later.

Certainly, Kennedy had his faults. He was over-confident, a five percenter, a womanizer, inexperienced at administration, addicted to painkillers, a bit of a hypocrite. At the other end of life, the positives, he was charming, well-read, urbane, brave, and cosmopolitan. When the Kennedys came to Washington, the cultural life of the city flourished on every level. From a drab, slightly quaint Southern town with no night life to speak of except the red-light district on 14th Street and the gin mills in Georgetown, it turned into a hot spot for music of all kinds, and the White House featured everything from avant-garde jazz to solid classical.

When Kennedy was assassinated, the world changed for millions of American teenagers. Many a teenage tear was shed that day, and many days more. The crying was not a political act. Something had been overturned, and nobody ever figured out exactly what. This question has not been resolved yet. It will never be resolved, and the ensuing grim wonder is part of the foundation of all that came after.

It has become *de rigueur* for younger generations to beat up on the Baby Boomers. This is not exactly fair. Whether right or left, this entire generation has a certain fixation on the Sixties. Their past is still alive. They can't help it. It was such a mixed-up decade, compressions of hope and despair, freedom and fear, danger glued to fantasy, a clash of cultures, prosperity and angst, war and peace, a flexion point of history, it was a battlefield of developmental values that are still being contested.

Since that time we went from one of the youngest Presidents in our history, a man who was headstrong, intelligent, inexperienced, urbane, witty, a man who loved people, to one of our oldest Presidents, headstrong, inexperienced, brash and cruel, divisive, a man who loves himself and thinks that humor consists in ridiculing others. We have come a long way downhill, and this is not a political statement.

<u>The</u> <u>Most</u> <u>Dangerous</u> <u>Politician</u> <u>in</u> <u>America</u>

The most dangerous politician in America is not Donald Trump. It is not Hillary Clinton. It is not Nancy Pelosi or Paul Ryan. It is not anyone who is dangerous because of ideas, the policy content of politics. The most dangerous politician in America is Mitch McConnell, and it has nothing to do with ideas.

It has to do with power, how you get it, how you keep it, and why. And it is because McConnell is so good at what he does, not because he has bad ideas or because he has any ideas at all.

It has frequently been noted about McConnell that, first of all, he represents the obvious. If you don't get elected, you don't get to make policy. You get to go home. So getting elected is the obvious thing to do if you want to make policy. This is a truism. The philosophy of power giving opportunity is not exactly front page news. It is both incredibly shallow and highly suspicious. Of course power gives opportunity. The question is what for, and spending most of one's time worrying about power causes the savvy observer to wonder most what the answer to "what for" is.

After saying first that he has to stay in power, McConnell says second that the most important job is to get federal judges appointed and confirmed, mainly circuit court judges. He does not say what these federal judges are supposed to do, but we can be sure that they are not just any qualified applicants. They are certain qualified applicants that agree with him on legal philosophy, but he does not specify which philosophy. Clearly their judicial tenor must accord with the notion that power comes first, and then opportunity.

McConnell is on record as saying that if his philosophy works, the federal judiciary he gets confirmed will be in control of national jurisprudence for decades to come. He is on record as saying, inasmuch as he controls the process of confirmation, he will use it only to bring judges up for confirmation that he agrees with. His is definitely not the policy of the most qualified applicant. He did this before with the Merrick Garland nomination, about which he is justifiably proud on his own terms, and he will do it again and again as long as he can, politicizing the judiciary.

He wants to rig the game. He is not the first, and without doubt he will not be the last, but he is definitely the best. This is precisely why he is dangerous. It is not because of his ideas, about which he rarely says enough to judge, but because of his use of power. Power gives opportunity, as we all know.

PRETENDING TO BE STARS

The basic itch is there the whole time under the skin,
The cranky style of life, the wonder that lost its luster,
And all the other brittle moods that saddle you up
And ride you down and complain that you buck
Too hard for the living room. The television drones on
Dispensing all the useful things to know in
The age of knowing everything and all the angles
When knowing nothing is the best knowledge of them all.
Is it zen or is it just the meditative fatigue of the tired
Old wisdom of the captive self? What the hell
Was Descartes thinking, the damn fool
Discovering the self? We could have lain with the cows
And chewed our cud if we knew what a cud was to chew.
The dogs would have barked at the hedge rows, where
The mysteries lie in wait for the dogs to bark,
And chased the butterflies. Our feet are too big
To chase the butterflies and they know it and this is why
The butterflies are gone, all gone and slipped away down
The gnarly hole with the fireflies who said every one that
They would not light our evenings any more because all
The fun went out of pretending to be stars in
The heavens on earth.

DEATH OF A LOVED ONE

Long before the Kangol cap was a known entity,
When all the Kangol caps were made of plain old felt
And never a snap on the brim, the brim was sewed on,
Upon a time there once was a maiden
Who knew what to do when somehow you gave
Your Kangol cap what looked like a fatal injury,
A ragged gash from the temple to the crown.
It does not suffer injuries well, felt does not,
Because the warp and woof of it were never there
And sewing it looks like trying to glue pieces
Of Jello together. So it seems to the rank amateur.
In the place where I somehow managed to inflict
This gruesome injury on my treasured Kangol cap,
As I stood there staring flummoxed how
To wear my Kangol cap that could not be worn
In this condition, this fair maiden took it
Gently from my hands and said,
"Let's see what we can do with this."
And she had a magic machine with magic thread
That would sew exes down the length of the mortal wound
And make it whole again and verily she did make it whole

Again, and it was just like new except for the neat scar
On it that looked like a plastic surgeon had put it back
Together like it should have been in the first place.
The name of this fair maiden was Leslie Fuller
And everyone who knew her
Will know what I am saying.

Mission Creep in Vietnam was the Intention

As a country under Donald Trump, we have returned to a defense policy vis-à-vis North Korea that is sixty-five-five years old. After fighting to a stalemate under Truman, national defense policy under Dwight D. Eisenhower was to commit the military globally to economic change, and if this did not work, to apply sudden and immense military action at a concentrated point.

All this was abandoned by the Kennedy administration in favor of the doctrine of "flexible response," a theory that lacked clear definition as well as a probative test. In Vietnam, the object lesson applied by Defense Secretary Robert McNamara was the Cuban missile crisis and the stand-down by the Soviet Union. Since there was no clear and absolute starting point as there was in Cuba, the strategy would be gradual pressure with the intention of turning up the heat when feasible. In other words "mission creep," which has long been considered the regrettable side effect of a strategy without a clear objective, was actually the McNamara plan from the beginning.

The Pentagon never signed on to this way of doing things. Military leaders like Curtis LeMay considered it madness, and the high command generally agreed with him, especially those directly involved in Vietnam planning and operations. Their thinking was either go in hard and get it over with or get out and wipe your hands. Later, after years of study, this was the general military lesson accepted, as we know from Colin Powell's assessment.

The civilians in charge, McNamara and Secretary of State Dean Rusk, never actually said what they wanted or how they wanted to do it. And Rusk expressed the mystifying opinion that the United States must keep on doing what it was doing, if the rest of the world were to trust American resolve. He was still peddling this line of bull decades later, after McNamara finally realized the gross error of the Vietnam adventure. The world does not trust American resolve yet.

It is not that gradualism is wrong necessarily, or that the quick-strike option is right. It is that clarity is necessary, and confusion is the first enemy. It was never clear what the Eisenhower considered grounds for a quick strike; we dallied around in Vietnam directly since 1956. It was never clear what McNamara intended, since he told so many people so many different stories. In other words, he told the truth when it was convenient, which is another way of calling him a liar, which he was. And now we have Trump, who thinks it is necessary to conceal his intentions until he acts, which is another definition of being unaccountable and reckless.

GROWING PEACHES IN NOME

Amazing the autumn falling upon
The leaves the trees still cling to,
Half still green, the other half all mixed, red
And yellow and pink and brown and orange
Like nectarines that lay out in the sun
Too long and got a little too randy
With the microbes, and the third half all brown
Below, flat on the ground for the birds to pick
Between, thrashing through the litter squirrels
Run crazy in for acorns, hazelnuts
And hawberries all shriveled now and dry.

The weather got confused, and the winter
Fell in love with the summer. The ice cream
Melted in the grocery bag when beer
On the back porch always kept icy cold
In cases. For Thanksgiving you warmed up
Your eggnog to drive off the chill and now
You need a frozen daiquiri to keep
The sweat off your brow the inclement heat
Was putting you through. Damn the climate change,
We'll just grow peaches in Nome Alaska.

LOVE TAKES COURAGE

When you're on a roll, keep placing the bet.
The day the ghost the give-up does his best
To do in its entirety you quit.
The plain and simple myth of it, legend
Before the truth, beyond the reckoning.
A reckless claim for sure when the science
Outweighs the comedy the Hamlet played.
The science? Love is in the air the ghost
Breathed out and left the rain to wash out clean.
You place your bet before you get your cards.
The truth will put your eye out, why you watch
To duck it when they throw it at you. Cold
It is like ice they make on the surface
Of Mars before they stage the play they stage
To prove that wanting is a pretty fool's game,
Exactly why when you're on a roll
You keep it going, keep reality
At bay and suck it up. Love takes courage.

<u>Why</u> <u>Does</u> <u>the</u> <u>South</u> <u>Want</u> <u>to</u> <u>Rise</u> <u>Again?</u>

Surprisingly, this question was given juice by the recent controversy over Roy Moore's closet sexual peccadillos. In his home state of Alabama the exculpations have been more over the top than Moore's own reaction, a predictable claim that the issue was a Northern liberal conspiracy to defame him. Never mind that Moore has done more over the years to defame his own self in the eyes of liberals than any wild-eyed radical could cook up if he was head saucier in the devil's kitchen.

After evangelical religious tropes about Joseph and Mary, Zachariah, and other Biblical May-December matches were splashed around Alabama to varnish over Moore's dalliance with a girl just fourteen, then intellectual apologetics from other Alabama sources came up to justify the Biblical arguments without claiming to validate their relevance to Moore.

Shot through it all is a longstanding defensiveness about the North common to the South, the suspicion that a godless Northern liberal press was always devoted to degrading Southern Christian evangelism. H. L. Mencken notwithstanding, this is stretching the truth all out of shape. Moore claims that God himself selectively negates the Constitution, a legal theory found more in the South than the North. Northerners find it seditious, and Moore deceptive and vaguely dangerous.

Adherents to this theory believe that they can pick and choose which statutory and Constitutional laws to follow, since they are all secondary to divine law. Saying so has the color of religious observance. In any case, the right to act according to this view is held to be God-given, personal, and beyond the law to constrain.

It is easy to see how this position resembles the justifications of the Confederacy. If one views the Civil War as a mythic cultural clash, then evidence for "Southern" flouting of "Northern" law is still above water today. Retrograde Southerners bristle at the suggestion that their cause was a bad one, whether the deficit was the North's superior economy or God's decline to support the South in war.

The iconic nature of the dispute is exampled by the elevation of a seldom-used naval flag to the main Confederate symbol, creating an emblem of ongoing grievance and an over-ripe claim to Southern pride. This particular symbology rose up as a rejection of the Supreme Court decision Brown v. Board of Education, an opinion ratifying law above belief and the power of central government over local will. The political story of this flag, unfurled in protest and waved in injured pride, gained prominence in 1954 as a novel, not a traditional, symbol of defiance.

<u>The Can-do Spirit: What Happened?</u>

For a century and a half, from America's industrial awakening to the opening of the third millennium, the one aptitude that every other ethnic group held the Americans famous for was the can-do spirit. It's a simple thing *in toto*. If it needs doing, we'll find a way. In the particulars it's extremely complicated, so many different things having to be done in so many different ways.

In the first instance, mastery of the can-do spirit entails confidence. Second, it demands experience with handiwork, calluses on the hands, and courage in the face of things that will bark your knuckles and make you bleed when you put a wrench to them. It started with hard work, on the farm and in the small town in a New World where the traditions had to be made from scratch.

It seems at first that it applied largely to the men but this would be a mistake. Tammy Wynette said, "Stand by your man" and what she was saying was widely misunderstood. She was saying that if you don't stand by your man, he would be sure to screw up, probably sooner rather than later. It is conveniently forgotten that these New World pioneer farm women had muscles and stamina and hands accustomed to kneading bread, doing laundry, milking cows and splitting kindling, not to speak of chasing after the children.

One of the attributes of the can-do spirit is imagination. In the old world of carbureted engines, if the linkage gave out and the engine couldn't get gas, you could fix it with baling wire and bubble gum if you knew how. This is not a joke. It can be done and has been. This is one of the things that all the other armies in Europe during World War II noted about the Americans. If it had to be done, they would find a way. The other thing was generosity. If time and effort had to be donated, they would get it done. They were generous in every way. Every other Allied army in Europe robbed and stole from the local populations mercilessly. The Americans gave away their chocolates and, what's more, their cigarettes.

The can-do spirit persisted through the seventies, but somehow by the nineties it had all but disappeared. Part of it was the disdain of youth for physical labor. If you had calluses on your palms, you were either a fool or a patsy. However, this fails to explain it. No member of the generation whose fathers fought World War II actually thought physical labor was the way of the future, and they were not surprised that their boys had no use for it, or that their girls had little interest in baking brownies and sewing furbelows. It was still a mystery how quickly the can-do spirit disappeared. The question is, Where did it go?

HALF-DRUNK, A SHIT-EATING GRIN

You thought that people you loved you would know
Forever. Half-drunk, a shit-eating grin.

The gutter makes a bad pillow, the curb
Is worse, the crick in your neck permanent,
Recurring every time you take a nap
End down, the bottle in the nightmare,
The dream dissolving.

The skid is better than the fall, less firm
And more absorbing, entertainment caught
In motion. Skill is out of place. The grin
Is crooked, comedy fat, humorless
The laughing, stays inside the open lips.

The friends they live, they live, they live in death.
You never said what you meant to say. In death.
You say it. In death you meant to say it.
In life you forgot. You thought of something
Else, you did not think, you meant to think it
But you did not know what it was. The curb

Is your pillow, you made your bed in concrete.
You could not know it would be like this.

The funny stuff betrayed you. How in hell
Were you supposed to know the time was right?
The time ended before the time was right.
The time was right when it made no difference.
The curb is a bad pillow, the gutter
A better bed, hard as concrete it is.

(Written with Reid Diamond in mind.)

WHO GRIMACED AND WHO GRINNED

The crazy way of seeing it is right.
To tell the truth right off the bat, the more
You holler, less is more. The pigeons strut
The sidewalks, pluck the stones just like the seeds.
You wonder when the heart, the eye, the gut
Turns inside out.
                        Before your eyes the light
Goes down. The geese go wandering in weeds,
Sit down when wind blows them sidewise, the eggs
Exposed, along the river path the dregs
Of last year's flood.
                        In time beyond the lore
Of city lights the cry of heaven beckons.
Who listens to such nonsense? Must be wind
Or may be madness. Time will tell who runs
Which way. Who stops.
                        Who grimaced and who grinned.

Thirty Years of Lies and Mistakes

For thirty years from 1960 to 1990 two American foreign policy adventures colored and upended world politics in ways that could neither be ignored nor resolved. Some of the American administrations specialized in lies and some in flawed judgment, but in both cases the outcomes were bad and permanent.

This period in history started out with the Vietnam War, an error in judgment by both Eisenhower and Kennedy that the Cold War could be fought and settled in Southeast Asia. Under Kennedy this rapidly turned into dissembling by Robert McNamara, who concealed the actual war policy equally from the public and the military. The deception increased with Lyndon Johnson making war policy decisions according to the effect on his 1964 Presidential campaign.

When Richard Nixon ran for and won the Presidency in 1968, the lying continued. He hinted at bringing an end to the war at the same time as he was increasing troop strength. When he escalated the war until two out of three American people disagreed with it altogether, political dissonance became complete, and much of an entire generation of young Americans grew up detesting their government. The rest of the world agreed with them.

Iran was the second error. By failing to secure the grounds and building of the American Embassy in Teheran, the Carter Administration allowed a gang of state-sponsored focus-group street hoods to take it over and hold the staff hostage. It was not too long after this that operators for the Reagan Campaign negotiated with the government of Iran not to release the hostages until after the coming election. Reagan won, and the eventual upshot of the episode was a criminal drugs-for-weapons conspiracy operating out of the White House.

America's reputation, already disfigured by numerous foreign escapades from Vietnam to Chile to Grenada, went in the trash. If not for two surprise events, one global and the other local, who knows how badly confidence in the United States might have degraded. However, the Soviet Union did collapse, and Iraq did invade Kuwait. The world's attention shifted, and the American instinct to assume the role of a global police force was acted out and, incredibly, more or less accepted. Adverse reaction from the Muslim world was predictable, and the equally predictable American counter-reaction was to double down, a tactic sure to fail.

Over two decades later, we are the global police still, without a mission or a clue. We are still lying about what we do, and this is still bogus.

<u>Drug</u> <u>Dealing</u> <u>and</u> <u>the</u> <u>Hard</u> <u>Line</u>

People who believe strongly in harsh penalties for drug dealers usually know nothing about drug dealing or the drug life. It is a feeling they have that something hard ought to be done, that drugs are being pushed on kids, and that harsh penalties will somehow convince the dealers to get out of the game. After the ignorance, these people are most of all angry.

Angry about drugs is an easy thing to be. It is not like it is some kind of rare or profound feeling. In fact it is common and understandable. The farther away you are from first-hand experience the easier it is.

The first misunderstanding about street drugs concerns the economics of supply and demand. The pressure for drug sales comes from the demand side of the equation, not the supply side. Users are saying "yes" to drugs; "just say no" is patent nonsense. The second misunderstanding is the introduction to street drugs. It is usually done by friends, and it usually comes after gradual experimentation.

In the suburbs the drug dealers are other kids, starting with the kids who have enough money to afford buying in quantity. Usually, they have found their contacts by initially driving into the inner cities as buyers and gradually upping the quantity. The only way you can drive into the inner city is to have a car to drive, meaning that your parents have enough money to buy you one. The inner city dealers are not driving out to Volvo suburbs to "push" drugs on kids. The dealers are the resident kids with money. They know that drugs don't have to be pushed on their friends. They want them already.

I sat on a drug murder jury where the foreman knew absolutely nothing about the drug world but considered himself an expert on it. He thought that his job was to bully the rest of the jury into accepting his opinions generally and, specifically, a conspiratorial theory of the murder. What he actually succeeded in doing was forcing a three-eyewitness open-and-shut case to a mistrial by hung jury, because the defendant was "obviously a nice boy who had been framed by drug dealers." There was precisely zero evidence to support this theory. He would certainly be tried again, the prosecutor told me wearily afterward. After all, he had blown the victim's neck in half with a shotgun at point blank range.

Confidence had got the foreman his jury position, but his anger and ignorance were counter-productive. It didn't help in the jury chamber any more than it helps in the court of public opinion.

The Evangelical Christian Fantasy

It is not that they believe devoutly in God. It is that they are certain God believes in them and all that they believe in.

The evangelists believe that Roy Moore's accusers are lying, when they cannot possibly know this. The very same evangelists turn around in the next breath and condemn Moore's critics of making deals with the devil. This is something else they cannot possibly know, unless perhaps they know the devil too. Believe you me, they are not making metaphors when they talk about the devil. To them he is as real as God is.

God whom they cannot possibly know, because God is too big to know. This is the entire concept of God, that which is too big to be known, and Saint Anselm's proof of his existence. Defining anything is a means of setting limits on it, and humans are incapable of defining God's limits. God is that than which nothing greater can be imagined. The greatest thing that can be imagined is by nature beyond comprehension. Every human being (other than the bona fide kooks) can imagine something so big his mind cannot get around it.

So saying that you know what God is, or the Devil, or what is in someone else's mind is a complete and utter fantasy. It is an appealing fantasy to those who are confident in their own minds. Of course, being confident in yourself is somewhat lower on the scale of comprehension than being confident in God's knowledge. So listening to evangelicals wax proud and loud is for some of us a lamentable exercise in patience. Moore's supporters have at times been outrageous in their comportment. Thursday an evangelical talking about millions of good women turning their attackers in to the police in real time, shouting down every other commentator who tried to speak, caused a television station to shut the segment down. His claim was that forty years time invalidated Moore's accusers

It is even lamentable at times listening to some of Moore's evangelical critics. A. R. Bernard, for instance, on television yesterday started in with the loud and confident exercise of his belief that the problem with the accusations against Moore is the lack of due process. Disregarding due process is fundamental to the American creed, he was maintaining. This was not only an improper conflation of culture and law but also a misunderstanding of due process itself. Multiple unforced and uncompensated public testimonials by unrelated persons is direct evidence, ipso facto. They speak to ethical considerations, not legal ones. For ethical considerations, credibility is the test, not preponderance of evidence or beyond a reasonable doubt.

<u>MacArthur</u> <u>and</u> <u>the</u> <u>Korean</u> <u>Holocaust</u>

General Douglas MacArthur is known for many things. A long and storied career and the author of many controversies, big and small, the object of great praise, mostly overdone, and the subject of much criticism, mostly on point. The thing that he is most famous for, and most infamous too, is the Korean War and being fired by President Truman.

The least known bit concerns the Korean War and the worst thing he did in that conflict, or anywhere else, the bombing campaign thought to have killed two million North Koreans, roughly ten per cent of the population. The story was not widely covered in the American press, nor would it have got much attention if it had. The Korean War was a cog in the American stand against Communism, and North Korea was its easternmost extension. The American jingos like McCarthy saw a Communist under every bed and in every closet. Bombing North Korea to a greasy spot on the map was in their program.

You can believe that the North Koreans have not forgotten about it. Their economy has yet to recover from it.

In MacArthur's defense, a difficult job for someone who sees more of the vainglorious in his life than anything else, plus a little administrative expertise, he was following the prevailing theory of war at the time. It was the theory of war, holding civilian populations hostage to destruction and economic collapse, that would predominate until the end of the nineteen fifties. It had been the theory of World War II and its precursor tests like the Spanish Civil War and a couple of South American wars. The benefit of it was considered twofold, ruined economies being unable to support their armies, and demoralized armies preoccupied with worry about their families.

It was mainly accomplished by strategic bombing, but the only time that strategic bombing was ever proved to work were the nuclear bombs dropped on Japan. Nonetheless, it was the theory of war propounded all through the Eisenhower Administration, and it was still being practiced in the Vietnam War—carpet bombing and chemical deforestation—neither of which accomplished the desired result, retirement of the enemy.

None of this excuses MacArthur's campaign in Korea any more than it excuses the destruction in Southeast Asia and the condemnation of thousands to chronic life-threatening disease from exposure to Agent Orange, including American boys.

<u>Putin</u> <u>and</u> <u>the</u> <u>End</u> <u>of</u> <u>Civilization</u>

There is something vaguely troubling about the Russian bombing campaign in Syria, aside from the things that are terribly troubling about it and the callous wanton disregard for civilians that it is. Callous wanton disregard for civilians is nothing new, however heinous it is.

Certainly it is nothing new for Putin's Russia. Annihilation and depopulation campaigns are sewn into the cloth of recent Russian history. During the Second Chechen War, Grozny, the capital of Chechnya, and several other Chechen cities were razed to the ground and completely depopulated, making refugees of several hundred thousand people, including many ten thousands of ethnic Russians. Numbers killed are hard to estimate but thought to be around a hundred thousand, one out of eight people, or more than twelve per cent.

Several of the weapons used in this and other campaigns in the Caucasus, southern Russia, and Ukraine had very little purely military value. They were designed to control or eliminate civilian populations. Thermobaric bombs, for instance, utilize atmospheric oxygen to produce a pressure front; some types produce fireballs also. Their purpose is to induce high-pressure blast injuries first and, when they are dropped en masse in cities, to create widespread conflagrations. An instant city on fire, in other words. Thermobaric bombs have been dropped on Syrian cities.

By itself, it is heinous, but also part and parcel of the Russian/Syrian strategy, which is to annihilate cities that could possibly support anti-Assad forces and depopulate regions that are sympathetic to the insurgent causes. It is an old military strategy, going back centuries in Central Asia, northern Europe, the Mediterranean Basin, Mongolia, and the "discovery" of the New World, as well as being the main theory of war during the twentieth century. So, however horrible it is, it is not novel, and terrorizing the citizenry is and has been commonplace in Africa, South Asia, and the Middle East by many different actors, both foreign and domestic.

The thing that seems to be different in Syria now is a comprehensive campaign to destroy hospitals. Targeting hospitals has been done from time to time in every war, but pervasive plans to destroy medical infrastructure open up a qualitative difference in warfare. It makes barbarity the intent and gratuitous destruction the aim. In short, it holds civilization itself as the enemy. It consists in being deliberately uncivilized. Killing is one thing; for the dead, there is no more pain. Purposely injuring civilians and then making it so they cannot be treated goes by the name of sadism, or worse, if there is anything worse in the blood sports of war.

Nihilism and the Tea Party

From the beginning of the Obama Administration to the advent of Donald J. Trump, I worked across the street from the Capitol building. The place where I worked across the street from the Capitol was Union Station, one of the busiest buildings in the world. Any time any public demonstration took place there concerning, about, or against the federal government or its laws, Union Station was a hotbed of activity. Activists passed through after travel, used it as a rest station for demonstrations near the Capitol grounds, or the staging area, preliminary show point, and post-demonstration rallies for the demonstration factions.

'This is the Sixties all over again' was my first thought when the Tea Party (known now as the Freedom Caucus of the Republican Party) first rallied in our nation's capital. By this thought I am not referring to the ideology. I am talking about the feel and color of the crowd, the high percentage of people in costume, the inventiveness of the theater, the loud spontaneous chanting, the number of large signs and banners, the general agitation of the crowd, the prancing and strutting and showing off, the churlish edge, the implicit nose-thumbing at the onlookers, abusing the people whom they hoped to impress. Add to this the willingness simply to take over a public conveyance such as Union Station is, where people in their daily lives work, pass through, eat lunch, and shop, and to deliberately make their lives miserable during those hours.

In other words, just as the hippies did in the Sixties, they were marching not just to promote their causes and protest their political foes, but to denigrate the general public for not seeing things the way they did. The insult was clear and common.

There was another way in which they resembled the hippies. The tone of temerarity in expressing their anti-social opinions and the agitated state of the crowd's Brownian motion, like a liquid presenting the boil, had the feel of the *danse macabre*, the frenzy of the last wild party before the world ends in fire. Whether they meant it or not, the feverish pitch of the spectacles took on the look of a political apocalypse overlaid with phony populism, nationalist fever, and the irredentism of the "true American" represented by the actual Boston Tea Party. They were surreal, these events, amateur theatrics demanding to be taken seriously.

This is how the Tea Party resurrected the "Paris Burning" vision of business-as-usual futility. If you trample their vision of the future, they will make yours untenable. If you defile their "purity," they will terrorize you socially with their presence, because it is their duty as a minority elite to ridicule your ordinary pretensions. Never mind that their pretensions are as banal and commonplace as they come.

The <u>Hamlet</u>

If it had been up to T. S. Eliot wearing his critic's skullcap, Shakespeare's Hamlet would have been struck off the list of top-notch drama. At the moment of this revelation, it might be enlightening to recall that in his notes on culture, Eliot lauded the Mississippi River as a great moving stream of wisdom that could be conferred on the watcher by the simple practice of watching intensely.

For all his art, Eliot, like a thousand Shakespeare scholars short and tall, never figured out the hawk and handsaw line. Their explanations border on the preposterous and extend to the laughable, or both simultaneously, when the real answer is so simple that their collective shame ought to be immense. To admit not knowing entails being guilty of the meaning: You don't know a hawk from a handsaw, that is, you don't know your asshole from your elbow. A hawk is the flat plate that a plasterer carries his working mud on. Thus the metaphor of not knowing the difference between a hawk and a handsaw is not only artful poetry but intimate knowledge of life's work itself, the thing that flummoxes the scholar.

There are many such points in the poetry of the Hamlet and its sprawling difficult narrative movement. The best speeches in the play are pure melody and pointed commentary both, loaded with layers of irony, some characters delivering banality as if it were the wisdom of the gods and others ashamed at their limitations when they are simply spreading the wax with the honey out of diffidence. For instance, Polonius's speech to Laertes, often taken for grand understanding, is intended to be comical, concocting high virtue from mundane conclusions about ordinary social norms. And Hamlet, fishing around for a way to throw Ophelia over, manages to make the great gong of the universe shiver and ring.

The other genius of the Hamlet lies in the handiwork of the drama, the potentialities of theater itself. Polonius can equally be played broad, making it clear that he is a pompous old oaf, or subtle, making it seem like he is wise until the audience realizes that they have old relatives just like him, who get by on slick delivery when the package is worn-out and laughable. Hamlet can deliver the "To be" soliloquy angry, as Richard Burton did in the modern-costume version, wistful and mystical as Laurence Olivier did, or almost flat, depressive and emotionally degraded, as did Kenneth Branagh. The play itself could be staged as comedy, and the play within the play as slapstick, a farce depicting the folly of life.

Yes, Mr. Eliot, it is an untidy spectacle, lurching and uneven, disrespecting of the unities, but this is exactly what gives it its life, and its versatility.

<u>Value</u> <u>of</u> <u>the</u> <u>Hippy</u>

The hippy was the best and the worst of the twentieth century. Collectively, the hippies were undisciplined, inconstant, and thrilled with the mysteries when plain sight would have told them that the mystical was always out of reach no matter how close you get. At the same time they were generous in every way, from practical matters to idealistic vision, eager to seek out the spark in life, and determined that it should be anything but boring.

Despite the loathing heaped upon them by the good ol' boys and girls, the law-and-order fraternity's starship troopers, and their own parents, they changed American culture indelibly. They gave it color and broke it out of the love-it-or-leave-it conformism that would in time make narrow-mindedness the aim of all right-thinking two-fisted White Anglo-Saxon Protestants and their goal of designing American ideology to suit themselves, screw the misfits who wanted the Constitution to mean what it said.

At this time, two and a half centuries after the Declaration of Independence, and fifty years beyond the short-lived heyday of the hippies, some things taken for granted are hard to remember the beginnings of. Hippies changed fashion by wearing what they felt like, as long as it was colorful. They changed hair styles and brought facial hair for men back. They started the organic food movement, the back-to-the-land movement, the craft beer movement, the hand-made cheese movement, the holistic medicine movement, the save-the-Earth movement, the natural beauty movement, etc. They changed the colleges by challenging their professors to explain, and they changed their parents by challenging their sincerity.

They changed music forever, not simply with rock and roll and blues and rhythm and blues, and the two-guitar, bass-and-drums bands, but by taking it out of Tin Pan Alley and putting it in the garage. Music exploded all over the Sixties, and it has not stopped yet. It has just evolved. The music had energy and drive and feeling and most of all, honesty. Some of it was bad but little of it was boring.

"Hippy" eventually became a term of derision and with good reason. The remnant long-haired pot-smokers in the Eighties were as likely to be petty thieves and low-lifes as anything else, mumbling nonsense and taking pride in ignorance. The old real hippies sold out their clothing boutiques, organic farms, craft breweries, and communes for good money. The hippy chicks had long since discovered the virtue in husbands with high-paying jobs. A home mortgage gives focus to the household budget. They became part of the American way that they had transformed.

The Dionysian Temperament

It was not bacchanalian, although that is how its critics saw it, and it was not utopian, although this is how its adherents wanted it.

In the Sixties the Dionysian Temperament took a foothold on American culture for a while. Usually it has been contrasted with an Apollonian Ideal, pitting Apollo, the God of Light, against Dionysos, the God of Wine. These two figures represent disparate ideals, but the question is how telling the metaphors are.

Apollo and Dionysos are loving brothers. Apollo represents harmony, order, and reason, Dionysos inspiration, ecstasy, and freedom. He also represents fertility, i.e. the celebration of sex. Dionysos represents theater, Apollo poetry, the one a public spectacle, the other an occupation of solitude. In the Sixties, a large proportion of youth went for Dionysos in a big way. The biggest way was the explosion of freedom from conventional mores in a conformist society, and naturally this entailed the exhilaration of sex.

It was not just that they enjoyed sex and seemed to have more of it, it was that they admitted it freely, extolled its curative virtues, and proselytized the practice. The promotion of sex was simply too much for the generation of their parents, and too little for the inter-generation of cousins, aunts, and uncles, who felt left out.

The counter-culturals went overboard with the hedonism and the part that frightened society most of all, mind expansion and the psychedelic drugs. They gave hallucinogens to people who were unprepared for them. Unlike the other drugs, seen as merely dangerous, the psychoactives horrified the general population. Beyond revolutionary, the complaint was, they destroyed the common belief system in a solid world, inducing mental illness. Evil crackpots took them.

The Dionysian reaction to critics was to condemn alcohol, undeniably the most dangerous drug in America, then, before then, and still now. More people are harmed by it than all other drugs combined, by a wide margin. However, alcohol is the staple intoxicant of the central culture. If you kick straight at "the system," you break your foot. People who make the laws drink alcohol.

Psychedelic drugs and drugs like marijuana became part of the American culture, to the chagrine of conservatives. The irony now is that the big investors in medical marijuana at the moment are three-piece suit wearing traditionalists, in it for the money.

I WISH I KNOW THERE IS

I wish I wish I wish upon a yard
Where I were you and you were I and love
Was in the grass like blankets of flowers
And silence was a passion in the wind.

I know I know I know your magic touch.
It speaks a language only known by you
And me of course and us like prayers unknown
To all the books diviners horde like gold.

There is there is there is not one but all
And who would say they understood the sun
In passing on until the tender night.
It wraps us in the dark so warm it lives.

FACING THE SEA

Windows facing the sea, the house is new.
People started building the new houses
About a hundred years ago. Old homes
Are weather beat. Wind batters the sea side.
Nothing to see out there. Gray waves and gulls.
All the jobs face the land where the door is.
The wind blows toward the jobs. Coming home
Is hard to do in the wind. People stopped
Working. The wind was slowly killing them.
They wanted something other than the wind
Killing them day after day for centuries.

They packed their bags one by one and moved out,
Trudged along the dusty roads. When they found
The wind no longer pushed them on, they stopped.
The people who found their houses built new.
They wanted windows facing the sea. Jobs
Were nothing to them. The sea was all
They wanted to look at. They were idle,
They had time to look, they had all the time
The sea had to give. They wanted to watch.
The wind was nothing to them but a nuisance.
They drank scotch while they looked out the windows.

<u>Real</u> <u>Compared</u> <u>to</u> <u>What?</u>

Reality is not a place or a thing—what the philosophers call a quiddity—a moving screen or a metaphysical form, a sensation or an impenetrable mystery.

Reality is an event. Reality has to happen—not just be there—in order to be real.

It requires a time and a place and it requires an observer, an intelligent observer. A place has things in it and time has changes and the observer has eyes, ears, a tongue, and skin. Reality can always be penetrated but it is not always the same.

A bunch of abstractions does not help to make it clear.

One of the early anthropologists in New Guinea once decided to take one of the remote hill people into a town so that he could see what the modern world was like. After they returned, he interviewed the man to see what his impression of the modern world was like, insofar as he could understand it. The hill native's answer was, "I did not know that a man could carry so many bananas." He had seen stevedores loading bananas onto a commercial packet for shipment overseas. Of the rest, it had not even registered. He was not equipped by experience to understand what it was, and therefore he did not see it; it meant nothing to him, and therefore it was not real. For the anthropologist, of course, it was real. It was real because he knew how to see it. He perceived the meaning of it.

If an Inuit takes you out on his daily business, what you see is a vast expanse of indistinguishable white snow, but this is not the reality. It is what you see but it is not the reality. The Inuit recognizes twenty different kinds of snow on the ground, and he has twenty different word-constructions for it, filtering the world and categorizing the reality. You cannot see this because you do not know how to see it. You could learn but it would take time. The Inuit knows it instantly.

If an Ituri pygmy from the Congo jungle takes you and the Eskimo out into the forest, all the two of you see is an impenetrable mass of different colors green. You have no idea what lurks there. The pygmy is listening to it, smelling it, feeling the atmospheric changes, studying the trail in front of him and the branches overhead. Seeing through the trees means little to him. It is not reality but he understands the reality of every smell, sound, and every mark on the ground and on the bushes.

Reality is an event requiring an intelligent seer and the seen. It is not fixed. It is the strangest thing in the universe, as well as the most common.

Is Donald Trump Unfit?

Is he unstable? Clearly. The lability, emotional responses out of proportion to the stimuli, is evident. Is he clinically ill? Probably. There is no question that his attention always turns to himself, evidence of narcissism, and his paranoia, seeing enemies in anyone who does not recognize greatness in him, itself a symptom of disorder, plus his inability to forgive any slight, are signs of psychological dysfunction. Without clinical testing, these cannot be established. Is he incompetent? It depends on which definition of competence is applied.

Is he qualified to be President? So far he has not shown that he is really good at anything but bluster and system-degradation. Has he shown that his capacities are acceptable and his decision-making functional? Clearly, he has shown that his administrative skills are substandard, and that his understanding of the legal powers of the Presidency is improper and barely Constitutional. Is he a leader? He is an extremely capable rabble-rouser. If the country can be run on the backs of the rabble, Donald Trump is in the running for the greatest of all time.

Is he unqualified? Maybe the better question to ask is, is he what the American people expect a President to be like. Most likely, two thirds of the people think he is not what they expect a President to be. Is the undying support of one third enough? It depends largely on who that one third is. If the bigoted bloc of the voting polity inhabits the one third—one third is absolutely not enough.

Generally speaking, the people expect their President to care about them, to be fair, to behave with decorum, and to demonstrate at least a passing knowledge how government works. On these counts, it would be hard to claim that Mr. Trump does anything but fail. The only real question is the degree of failure.

His emotional character could best be described as antipathetic. He is quick to anger and slow to show mercy. He barely responds with compassion to victims. He bullies critics when possible. He will absolutely not accept responsibility for any failure. He exacts revenge for criticism when he can. He has picked as cabinet secretaries people who are inimical to the aims of their own departments.

His prior reputation is not a good one. He partnered with thugs and shysters, sent his children out to commit felony sales fraud on one property, Trump SoHo, and he sued banks he owed money to, the reason no American bank will lend to him. He cost casino investors near a billion dollars, yet he took the tax loss credits. Given who some of those investors were, he is lucky to be alive. Our President, for now.

<u>What</u> <u>is</u> <u>Reality?</u>

If you were to ask members of any Western society what reality is, basically, most likely the answer would be something that can be touched, or seen, something that has a mass and a surface area. Even the metaphors that we use to describe thoughts and sensations refer back to physics in one way or another: That is a weighty idea. This is a deep thought. The other is a bright shining hope.

The word "matter" itself is a metaphor for wood. When the Greeks were searching for the way to describe the indivisible realities of the world, "wood" was the word they used to define solid matter, or to suggest a definition. They did not mean that every object in the world came from a tree. They just had to have a word to refer to all things solid, and wood was it.

The physicists, the people who study and define all things material, that is, fundamentally "wood", however, have long since told us that all materials are fundamentally porous. Everything material is made up most of all of spaces. In these spaces there exist forces that we understand the workings of. We can describe the interaction of these forces, and we can categorize the mechanics of their movement, and measure their effects, but we cannot say what they are.

We can say that if these forces ceased to exist, and the spaces collapsed between the subatomic particles, very large things would become very small. They would become so small that size would no longer have any meaning. The mass of a human body would be smaller than a speck of dust, but weigh the same. The earth would fit in a teaspoon. "Solid" reality mainly consists of spaces. The matter in it is unbelievably heavy, that is to say, massive but not big.

Some people think scientists can tell us what reality is, yet they have not been able to solve their own most fundamental question: What is the relationship between gravitation and the electromagnetic spectrum and thermodynamics? One does expect the definition of anything to encompass its most basic ingredients.

The other, fundamentally different, way to approach the question is to look at how babies find what is real and what is not. For babies, magic exists. You put the toy down where it did not exist in front of them and you take it away. Magic. Soon they learn it is not magic. They do not see well at first, because they have not learned to filter out the light waves that do not matter. Most of seeing consists in arranging the mind to see. The eyes receive light. The brain sees. The brain has to learn to see. The baby has to learn the reality. It has little to do with physics.

<u>CANDLES</u> <u>IN</u> <u>A</u> <u>SACRISTY</u>

Fluorescent streaks, like flame, like lava clouds
The sky belched out of nowhere, like a rip
In time the curtain spread and there was hell
Without the demons riding nags that snorted fire
And left the traces loose upon the evening sky.
Like liquid fire was thrown across the field
By armies upside down and downside up
The heavens breathing indiscreetly flame
So brightly unbelievable must be
A backlight, klieg light hanging in the sky
And ropes up there to tend it.

The darker it got, the brighter the fire.
The nothing turned, the black outgrew
The space, the universe turned inside out
And in the shadows fire got hotter, tore
The hole and sucked the fire into the sun
Below the line of memory. It glows mild
Like candles in a sacristy.

<u>Kafka</u>

The Kafka that readers of English know, the Kafka of the schoolchild texts is not the Kafka that wrote in German. Kafka was a Czech, and he wrote German as a second language. Numerous Czechs spoke German, especially in the north and west. German was an important language for an urban Czech to know.

German syntax and sentence construction are quite different from English, especially the English common in the twentieth century. The Germans love dependent clauses, and they put the main verb at the end to wrap up the sentence after stringing together thousands of dependent clauses, instead of putting the predicate in the middle of the sentence like any reasonable person would do.

Putting that insidious little joke aside, this difference makes learning German a difficult task to master, although it is valuable. Much great literature was written in German, and for some authors such as Kafka, reading it in the original language is a must. The first translators of Kafka did not render it into English faithfully. They created a whole new Kafka, who wrote in short crisp straightforward sentences about fantastic occurrences in such a way that the style belied the content. It intensified the gulf between the perception and the reality, the surrealism.

This, however, was not the way that Kafka wrote. Granted, all German is more complex than English, but Kafka wrote in a particularly oblique style, subtle and delicate, convoluted and indirect, more Robert Musil than Max Frisch. Perhaps it was because German was a second language, and he was struggling with the ideas and descriptions, or perhaps it had something to do with his extensive reading of Russian authors, as a Czech might, and the effect they had on his ideas.

In any case, <u>Metamorphosis</u> was not about a big bug. It was about someone who woke up feeling like some kind of vermin. It was the feeling of alienation, the psychological symptom of alienation and the problem of identity. <u>The Castle</u>, long held to be understood as a diatribe against bureaucratic society, was about that only as a matrix or a side issue. Kafka was writing about theory of knowledge: How do you know what you know and how can you prove it? The Castle is particularly boring in English; in German, not so much. It has suffered the same fate as Ortega y Gasset's <u>Revolt of the Masses</u>, being diminished by too literal an evaluation.

New translations of Kafka were undertaken a few years ago. One can hope they will be read widely, so that people can understand Kafka the way he wrote.

The Curious Case of Pocahontas

This is how the public indictment in the case lays out.

She has blond hair. She comes from Massachusetts. She inherited her status. Her last name is Warren, so obviously she is one of the Massachusetts blue-bloods, a member of the White Anglo-Saxon Protestant ruling class and a descendant of people who landed on the Mayflower. Clearly her claim to have Cherokee or Delaware native American heritage is ridiculous and laughable.

It is all wrong except for the hair color.

Her maiden name is Elizabeth Herring. She grew up lower middle class in Oklahoma City, Oklahoma. Members of her family have been Oklahoma residents since the 19th century. Picked at random, one of eleven residents of Oklahoma have Cherokee ancestry to some degree, and if you sort for other tribes, the chance becomes greater. If you sort for Oklahoma residency since the 19th century, the chance becomes even greater. Probably one in four persons born in Oklahoma to an old-line Oklahoma family have some native American ancestry.

So, Elizabeth Warren's claim to Cherokee and Delaware heritage is neither ridiculous nor laughable.

It is unclear in the particulars whether she has native heritage or not. The marriage records in Oklahoma for her direct family do not indicate that she does. This is not dispositive, however. Many 19th century Oklahomans denied Indian heritage, if they could, on account of the disadvantages and the shame it brought to them. Elizabeth Herring claimed that she had overheard relatives of her grandparents' generation talking about Cherokee and Delaware in the family. Briefly in her youth, she looked into claiming native heritage for financial assistance in college but abandoned the idea.

She has not undergone genetic testing, which her critics have found to be a denial of the claim. However, commercial genetic testing of the kind advertised on television would likely not be probative one way or the other. Such tests use virtual statistics, and they are not nearly as accurate as they are made out to be. A more narrowly targeted test might be probative.

Either way, it makes no difference. The claim has potential. It is not settled. And it is laughable to people who want to ridicule her for their own reasons.

EYES FROM DALI'S BRUSH

The new adventure coming up is death
Too soon before the work is done. The road
Is never paved. Macadam would be cross
To think his theory was mistaken, rocks
Don't fill the spaces. Asphalt does. In time
The washboards ruin the ride. Of course
When death pretends to be the end, the end
Is never reached. The road goes on and on
Until the car runs out of gas and soon
As that you find your mission barely known.
The holy grail has been discarded. Where
It is is secret. Dust has blown across
The road. The road looks like the open field.
The gas is gone. Adventure lies behind.
The work is done before it is laid out
Hard-boiled and second-rate, all cut and dried
And useless, sitting on the dust like eyes
From Dali's brush, staring at paradise.

DECEMBER......................

231

Civilization Comes from Women

Who did you think it came from? Babies spend the first three years of their life with women. This is how civilization started and this is how it still is. Even when they go to day care they are being tended and mothered. Their imprint on the way the world works is founded by women.

For their mothers the cause is love. For the babies the issue is milk. Babies have no way to feed themselves. This should go without saying, but not saying it is disregarding the most basic fact of early childhood. The mother is the stream of all things human and necessary. A woman is the first and strongest bond and the greatest teacher of the most basic terms of life and civilization.

Undoubtedly this is how it all started. In the beginning there was woman. In the very nascent stage of the evolution of Homo X, a mutant female with fully plantar feet, opposable thumbs, a bowl-shaped pelvic girdle, and a fully erect stance to support a huge cranium, held in her arms a little mutant baby that she realized with her large brain needed love and training. Little by little she taught her equally erect child, who could no longer climb into the tree canopy to save itself from predators, how to find food, perceive danger, and to band together with relatives.

Because the new human was fairly slow-moving it had to learn to use shelter to protect itself. Because it had opposable thumbs it could (literally) manipulate its environment. Because it had large powerful buttocks it could jog for miles and run down game by exhaustion. Because it had plantar feet it could balance an erect stance. Because of its nimble fingers it could throw a weapon accurately.

It needed to be able to communicate particulars. There is no question that this started between mother and baby in the very beginning. The rudiments of speech undoubtedly came between a mother and a baby. Then that baby became a child who communicated to other children, and over time the plastic capacities of the human brain took over and stored the knowledge, and culture, the mold of civilization, was born. It took thousands of years, but nothing succeeds like success. The new human was not the strongest or the fastest or the biggest, but it knew how to speak and plan and calculate, a tremendous advantage.

It started with a mother and a child. And it keeps on with mothers and children. Babies learn so much in their first years about the world and how it works that it is hard to categorize, since it is so basic. Women give life and they give civilization.

Note <u>to</u> <u>a</u> <u>Conservative</u> <u>Apologist</u>

Now Carl. If you had not doubled down on the carnage-metaphor gibbering, instead of saying in plain English what you meant, I might have been able to figure out whether or not I agreed with you on the ACA. I may not be a genius but I do know more than a little something about insurance and economics both.

I always liked the idea of universal coverage. I have to admit I was disappointed by the ACA. These omnibus bills are like putting everything in the cafeteria line on your tray. You may want it but you can't even carry it.

Its progenitors had invoked G. K. Chesterton's dictum: "If it's worth doing, it's worth doing badly."

It was unwieldy. It had too many moving parts. It required the invention of novel legal concepts like a penalty that was a tax. It had no provisions for investigation and enforcement. It did not address fundamental health care cost containment or the deficiencies of the federal fee-for-service model and consequent billing fraud epitomized by the current Florida governor's prior company. And when the talk came to insurance exchanges and subsidies, risk pools, outside line sales, and voluntary group insurance, the handwriting on the wall stood out clear. It could not last.

The health insurance stooges are the worst of the insurance racketeers. A Winnemucca casino is a paragon of virtue by comparison. This part of the bill was vulnerable by definition.

Still and all, it was well meaning, which is more than one can say about the AHCA and BRCA monstrosities, which are cruel double-talk, lacking any semblance of sincerity. Paul Ryan is on record bragging about the House bill being the first retrenchment of an entitlement in American history.

Health care has a moral dynamic as well as a practical one. It does have to be paid for on a sustainable line, but paying for it is a civic virtue. It's in everyone's best interest not to have a sick population.

<u>The Foreign Policy Craze</u>

Of the many current amateur military historians on social media, both on the left and the right, most are cracked. This is in addition to their being neophyte ideologues, having done just enough thinking to hold strong opinions without becoming knowledgeable enough to make seasoned judgment. Those on the left frequently find American foreign policy more reprehensible than that of any other nation, and those on the right confuse the will to power with sense.

It is no wonder that the current situation has the end spectra befuddled, since the left is adamant that the United States is the adversary and Russia the victim, while the right coddles Russia so that the Trump Administration can proceed unfettered. On this issue both ends come out the same. The left sees the Kim administration in North Korea as more moderate than the Saudis, and the right sees Iran as more of a threat to the West's stability than Syria. American reactions have gone topsy-turvy, and which side needs which medication has never been less clear.

It is absolutely true that, if the American foreign policy imperative had been to promote representative government around the world, it has been a deplorable failure. It has not always been certain that the promotion of representative government has been the aim, however. For many administrations it was the promotion of stability, and this has always augured well for autocracies, since a single man is easier to control than a society. Furthermore, as has been argued here and there, it would make little sense after the Civil War for the United States to foster self-determination around the world, when it denied self-determination to the South. How could it think better of the rest of the world than its own people?

There is a fanciful strain in American foreign policy, epitomized by Teddy Roosevelt, that nations could be judged the same way people are judged. Nations have good and bad behavior, they need to be encouraged or held back, they have emotions and impulses and character. They are mature or childish, in which case they need discipline from a parent country. This has led to the forced cession of Panama from Colombia, the occupation of many Latin American and Caribbean countries, and many a lame adventure disguised by flag-waving as glorious.

Another strain of foreign policy is cynical, coming from the domestic need to maintain power by showing strength overseas. This is especially damaging to good governance, both internally and abroad, because it has been accomplished by lies, big lies about aims and reasons and little lies about what and how from Chile to Vietnam to Korea. The resulting picture is neither pretty nor decent.

<u>The</u> <u>Liberal</u> <u>Paradox</u>

How did the liberal imagination go wrong in the United States?

After the American Revolution proved to the world, not that the vote was the cure-all for society's ills, but that geography itself should be the main frame for representation, ruling out genealogy, it took another century and a third to settle the test of aristocracy. This test was World War One, and the European aristocracies lost. Therefore their dominions around the world were eventually lost on the heels of their weakness, and World War Two severed them from their overseas control.

Out of this emerged the superior powers of the American state and its vast economic wealth. The United States represented over fifty per cent of the world's GDP. Nevertheless it had to settle its own internal divisions and determine what consensual national world-view it would adopt, since it did not have one shaped by centuries of tradition. Theirs was a new way of politics in action.

This is not an easy question to set out and study. What would the shape be of a frontier society now that it was settled, prosperous, and on top? Individualism was the preferred answer, the relic of the pioneer creation myth, Paul Bunyan sized down to suburban tract homes and the two-car garage. Could it be the reality?

What role would the schools have in resolving the matter by socialization? Post-World War Two, the elementary schools held competitions in the spring. Eventually, as it happens, each year a small number of students dominated. The school administrations said that this was wrong. Other children must get recognition. Eventually over a few decades they ceased giving out medals for winning, and all students got participation medals so that no one was left out.

It was a metaphor. America had decided by acclamation that a promise for equality of opportunity should be replaced by an effort to produce equality per se. The lesson for school students was that conformism would be the role model of social behavior. No one should stand out except as a representative of the school, and if you tried to stand out on your own, you would be cut down to size.

The individualism left over by the frontier experience remained as a relic in the mythology, however, and was never resolved to the conformism. The problem still dogs the American liberal, who has framed equality as a utopian leveling experiment while measuring liberty in dollars. They did it without delivering the chance of development from the bottom up, by making credit easy to get.

Fake News is Nothing New

In fact, in the United States fake news goes back to the founding of the Republic. In 1982 Benjamin Franklin published the infamous "Bag of Scalps" story, intending to inflame public opinion against the British, who were falsely accused of paying native Americans to scalp settlers, terrorizing them. Later Thomas Jefferson wrote a once-obscure but now-celebrated letter complaining about fake news in the mainstream press. At the time Jefferson knew full well that all the newspapers were political. After they made their money printing handbills and circulars and posters under contract, they were then free to publish any lies that suited their causes. They were all fakers, Jefferson's supporters as well.

By the 1830's, most of the newspapers, the "penny papers", had converted to advertising as their profit center, and therefore they tried to increase circulation any way they could, to generate revenue. They printed stories that would excite public interest in dropping a penny or two. In 1835 the New York Sun published a story titled "Life on the Moon" about a new and powerful telescope that could see the moon's life, and soon thereafter Edgar Allan Poe challenged it as a hoax, since the Southern Literary Messenger had published his "true story" that life on the moon had indeed been discovered by other means. (The Sun story had actually included a disclaimer at the story's conclusion that it was not true.) In 1844, in order to incite violence against the Irish, anti-Catholic Philadelphia newspapers were publishing fake stories about Irish thieves stealing Bibles from Philadelphia's schools. Fantastic published reports in the South had slaves spontaneously turning white, turning the actual white residents paranoid about their neighbors.

In 1874 the New York Herald featured a false story about a mass escape of animals from the Central Park Zoo. Many people were killed, allegedly. The real consequence was a public panic, causing the City authorities to step in. Later in the century, the Spanish-American War was touched off by a fake story about enemy sabotage of the U.S.S. Maine, an outdated gunship destined for the scrap heap. A steady stream of fake stories about Spanish atrocities against American residents fed the public outrage against the Spanish authorities in Cuba.

The Tonkin Gulf Incident, intended to justify direct military action against North Vietnam, was not merely fake news. It was a set-up. For weeks prior to the supposed incident, two American destroyers had been patrolling North Vietnamese territorial waters, firing on gunboats and shore installations, hoping for return fire.

The difference now is not the fact of fake news. It is the instant dissemination.

The Gender-specific Fallacy

Now that women have decided, and rightfully so, that they will refuse to be victims of unfair sexual mores, the argument is already being advanced that because they have been victims—because they know what moral inferiority is—we can take it for granted that they will understand by contrast how to be morally superior themselves in the face of temptation. Maybe this is true. Is the possibility sufficient to guarantee the argument? Does it necessarily entail any further conclusions, such as that women will forever after act right? After all, individual normal-seeming men did use power wrongly once they got it.

Moreover, it is also predictably being foretold that if more women were put in elected positions, government would run better. The reasons are the standard litany of the gender-specific superiority of women. They share more. They care more. They are better socialized. They are more gentle. They forego sexual oppression. They are familiar with compromise. They can organize without putting their egos in the way. Having had the primary care of children, they understand the hidden motivations of the human animal.

This hinges on one of the primary fallacies in ethics, comparing the good attributes of one thing with the bad attributes of another. Of course the good things about women are better than the bad things about men. Nevertheless, people who have had women as managers or bosses can certainly inform the world about the ways in which women are not universally superior, either socially or professionally.

Because women are not generally confrontational, however, it does not mean that categorically they are easier to deal with. They have other means of getting people to knuckle under. They form alliances. They divide and conquer. They whisper in the shadows. They concoct the did-you-hear-this campaign, whether what they heard was made-up or not. They ask subordinates versions of the "have you stopped beating your wife" question, like, "Is it true that you are not performing well because you do not feel confident you are capable of getting it done?"

Feminist theories of gender sociology, like that of Dr. Deborah Tannen, are usually careful not to make the outright claim that women are superior to men. They use code and emotionally-charged words, such as "share", "care", "join", "support", "communicate", and "non-confrontational" to imply the case. Women do need to be more involved in politics, and they certainly will be, just not because they are better people. It will be because they are equal to the task. They are half the population to be represented, they are essential, and we need them in the mix.

A LOAD OF CRAP

Oh why? I never knew the reason why.
The reason why the sun goes on around
The planet in the dark and captures light
To save for future days. A load of crap
They tell about the science in the wind.
The breezes blow and snow does fall and love
Does bind you to your loved one when you give
It freely. Give it and you have it, makes
No sense, makes all the sense you need it to.

A load of crap it is to have to make
When sense is nothing but a proof of what
You know already. Proof is what you make
Of idle time all busy with regret
And stars do shine when daylight fills the sky.
It is a reason made when all you do
Is dream of days when nothing fills the air
And doing nothing is the dream of time
And all you do. The reason soon dissolves,

The reason melts away and you the rest
Between the spaces, beating heart and time
To fill with what you see around you. Good
To be alive when wonder fills the day.

<u>Alabama</u> <u>Today</u>

What are we witnessing in Alabama today? Is it more than a greenlighting of bigotry, racism, xenophobia, reactionism, and religious intolerance? Is it a feeble tolerance of pedophilia as long as the perpetrator offers a thin tissue of denial? Is it the sorry delusion that slavery was merely a regrettable economic diversion best forgotten? Is nostalgia over the myth of a golden era for family—in fact an outright deception about slavery, debt bondage, child labor uncontrolled by law, women considered chattels, and an age of consent as low as ten—a desirable sentiment?

It is conveniently forgotten that the 19th century was a time when the age of consent to be married in these United States was ten in many jurisdictions. This is somewhat different from the age of consent to sex, but the lower the age of consent for marriage, the lower the age of consent to sex. Female children from larger poor families were often sold as wives and servants, meaning that pre-teen girls grew up knowing that they had been traded for money into *de facto* involuntary servitude. Is this anything that anybody wants to return to? Or is there a perverse hope buried in it somewhere that pedophilia itself can be vindicated?

Actually, it's an ancient Old World idea, a remnant of European aristocratic privilege. Until sometime in mid-19th century Europe, basically a member of the aristocracy could not be prosecuted for sex crimes. It was the prerogative of male royalty to take any woman or girl they liked, and it happened frequently in the countryside. There was no age of consent, since consent was not a requirement. This practice continued in rural Eastern Europe up until World War II, many decades after it had been discouraged effectively in France and Britain.

Overthrowing rule by men had been the exact formal reason for the American Revolution. Rule of law means that the courts cannot formally consider the status of an individual in making a legal judgment. Of course, status persisted, and still does affect judicial decisions in fact, but this is an informal consideration subject to the law, unlike the Europe of the aristocracies.

It's high time we forget the movie myths about the idyllic family life of the past when everyone was happy whistling while they worked. In fact it was a time when everybody knew their place and economic mobility was rare. Ostracism, if not tar and feathers, was the penalty for bucking the social order, and the only way to be shut of it was to migrate west. What conservatives in Alabama really want is the pipe dream of an un-American world where everyone agrees with them that rule of law is constrained by religion, their religion, of course, ruled by their men.

YOU KNOW

What did I expect to bring back from
The darkness? Does it matter if the mold
Scraped off the walls, forgotten in the time
It took distilling down the memory
Of toxic dust breathed in, and wafting out
And lost before the tragic firmament
Is sealed inside some bottle? Roiling smoke
Of marijuana fills the nose. In the gap
Between the sensible and all the rest
The question stays as open as before.
What did I expect to find there? The dark
Is changeless. Stumbling is the way of it.
What does it matter if the fall precedes
The find? The light does not exist. The things
Look different from the way you feel them. Hard
They are and common, known to all and seen
By few, the understanding hurtful. No,
The pain is gone. The magic in the truth
Was never in the bottle, corked or not
Or vapor in the air. What you forgot
You knew before you knew it. In the light
The seeing is reward enough. You know.

HOUSE OFF THE OLD ROAD TO FLOYD

A nineteen fifty seven Chevrolet
Was parked beside the house. A massive oak
Rained leaves on grass uncut for countless years.
A thousand children ran across the yard
In dreams and none had peeked between the boards
Or seen the shadows broken by the shafts
Of light that scintillated golden dust
From cracked-up windows down to creaking floor.

In the days when the memories were long
The tulips grew in rows and the roses
Beaded up with dew in the morning mists
And the goats jumped the fences in the rain
While the wind blew across the flapping gate
Unlatched. It was careless how the owners
Tried to manage from the rocking chairs kept
On the porch. All the dogs did run away.

The holler road was washed out in the flood
Last year. A long time gone was last year came
And went, near twenty year was last year gone
It came and went and stayed there in the flood
And the dogs ran away and took the goats
With them and on the porch, the chairs took still.
The peace took over from the stillness. Dog
After dog ran out from under the porch.

The Lost China Hand

Emmanuel "Jimmy" Larsen was eleven years old when his family moved to China. They had lost everything in the San Francisco earthquake of 1906, and his Danish father used a friendship at UC Berkeley with Sun Yatsen to get a position at the University of Chengdu teaching classics. This was how Jimmy ended up going to Chinese schools taught in Chinese while his older brothers and sisters went to missionary schools. When the Ching dynasty fell in 1911, they left China.

After graduating from the University of Copenhagen, Jimmy returned in 1916 to take a job with the Chinese Postal Service, a European consortium. Immediately, he was put in charge of building post roads into Tibet, the first modern highways into the high mountains. During his ten years in the Postal Service, he met and negotiated with nearly all the provincial leaders of the Warlord Period.

Upon leaving the Postal Service in 1926, he represented tobacco and wool interests in China until he was engaged by Chiang Kaishek as a secret agent investigating American arms sales to the Japanese through Chinese proxies. This lasted until 1935, when the head of the Japanese garrison in Beijing politely recommended that he return home to the United States for his health. Apparently an epidemic of Japanese army truck crashes involving Danish pedestrians had been predicted.

He bounced around for a while working as a consultant and translator before he was plucked from the Library of Congress by President Roosevelt himself to found a China Desk at Naval intelligence. From there he went to State to work at its China Desk. He donated open-source files gleaned from Chinese newspapers to both agencies. These two acts came back to haunt him after World War II.

The post-war anti-Communist hysteria was in full swing. Jimmy was a target, despite his own fervent anti-Communism. First, he wrote the analysis on the Chinese Civil War that concluded Mao was winning. In Washington this truth was taboo, and it put the messenger in jeopardy. Second, the Asia section at State was leaking like a sieve, and without a shred of evidence President Truman blamed Jimmy. Later, Truman was proven wrong. However, Jimmy had lent a couple of his open-source files, which had been classified unbeknownst to him, to the head of the Asia Society. He pleaded to a technical violation of espionage law.

A modest fine paid, and our foremost expert on Chinese leaders was ruined purely to satisfy the egos of sanctimonious politicians. When Jimmy died in 1987, his son refused to publish any of his writings. He had never read a word.

THE HOMELESS PAY NO TAXES

The grayest year on record, certified
By polling data gathered on the street.
The homeless pleaded for a break and watched
The politicians drooling, envious
Of change they held in soda cups,
And walking past they curled their lips and sneered
With all their might. Who were these people camped
On sidewalks poaching handouts? Jobs abound
For anyone who serves the dollar well
And proper. They are sinful, these poor slobs,
For giving up on life and saying no
To work but living in the luxury
Of idleness, leeching pennies when they could
Be giving dollars to the treasury
And paying salaries that are our right,
Their duty to support us in the fight
As legal representatives. Our right
As legal representatives. Our right.

<u>Why</u> <u>Current</u> <u>Middle</u> <u>Class</u> <u>Tax</u> <u>Cuts</u> <u>are</u> <u>Bogus</u>

There is a good reason why the tax cuts proposed in the new stealth tax reform bill do little for the middle class, and even less for the poor. None of these people make enough money to get meaningful tax relief, and when the proposed tax breaks are retired in a few short years, their tax burden will be larger than it was before.

The good reason why the tax relief is not meaningful is that it does not increase buying power. Buying power is the rise in income compared to prices. In a consumer-oriented economy, income levels must at least keep pace with the cost of living so that the people can spend how they want instead of how they have to. In short, how can wages be raised in a way that people have more discretionary income to spend? Discretionary spending is the margin of success. The real need, the economically real issue, is the upward movement of wages in relation to the declining value of money. This is the thing that is missing. People don't make enough money. Tax relief does not cure this problem.

To condense the question, how can the forty year old stagnation of wages be reversed? Real wages have stagnated since the early seventies. They have decelerated against GDP. They have gone up but not as fast as the value of money has gone down.

For instance, if a car had cost you twenty thousand dollars when you were making fifty thousand per annum, and five years later when you were making fifty-five thousand the same car cost you twenty five, you were losing money, not breaking even. The car cost twenty five per cent more but you were making only ten per cent more. This happened with respect to everything, so that when all the necessary items were bought, the things that you could choose to buy were fewer. The percentage of discretionary spending goes down as the necessary spending goes up, and using revolving credit to make up the difference is a losing game.

When the aggregated total of discretionary spending decreases, the national economy decreases in step with it. In a consumer economy, the best thing is the opposite, increased consumer spending. Real rising wages would increase spending, causing GDP growth and taxable revenue growth at the same time. The effect on taxation would be direct, and lowering the tax rate could be done without reducing the internal revenue, while increasing discretionary spending. The margin in discretionary spending is proportional to the growth of GDP. GDP growth is good for everybody. Real wage growth is good for GDP. It's as simple as it looks, paying people more money. It would even make the wealthy wealthier.

THE GOOD IN EVERYTHING

I wish I saw the good in everything.
Dear Lord. I wish I saw. I wish. I saw.
I yam what I yam, said popeye, and I
Said good-bye when you said hello, the raw
Deliverance of wealth in the honey
The bee imagines in the nectar. Yes,
The flower knows what it is doing. Far
Beyond the field, the pollen spread about,
Of course it does not know how that happens.
It opens up and spreads its depths because
It works. How could it know anything else?

Your lips are nectar and I am the bee.
You say hello and I say hello how
Are you? I like your taste, the honey comes
In close when I digest your smile. I read
Your color trip by trip and stop and light
So soft on petals drawing me inside
Where nectar raw and sweet lies pooled, the well
Too deep for me to drain, I never tire
Of trying. You are the life and I the way.
The good proceeds on its own sweet level.
It does not end when it ends. It goes on.

<u>COULD</u> <u>BE</u> <u>THEY</u> <u>KNEW</u> <u>SOMETHING</u>

The sky pale fuchsia all the way around
Horizon line then brilliant orange bulge
At dawning point streaking cross the dome
And pinking haze painted on the sunset side
Gray with clouds ominous. Then all dirty gray
Pale pink overwashed and streaks of gray blue
In between and then the gray blue won the war.
The pink retreated to horizon all way round
As sunset side the omens built up threatening.
A dirty blue took the dome as all the birds
Of every size flew north who knows why.
Could be they knew something we do not.
Took less than half an hour. The leaves
Unfallen have a bright gold shine.

The Original Sin of Democracy

It has often been said, or hinted at, that the American system has a dissociative disorder at its foundation, a schizophrenia. A split personality, if you like. Here you have history's hinge, a republic based on the vote and a representational system based on geography. No hereditary titles were recognized. It did not mean, however, that heredity was not recognized.

Here you also had slavery, based specifically on heredity. In fact and on the ground the friction between these two elements, representation separate from heredity and slavery based on heredity, has never been fully resolved. The problem with it and the fights over it still live in the body politic. White supremacy, although highly elaborated in some of its forms, is strong as ever, and the black reaction is more impatient than ever. The first is difficult to comprehend, while the second is easy to understand and difficult to see why it has taken so long to break out.

The original sin is a national disgrace, and yet the nation's most injurious war was fought over it without settling it, another conflict that has not only never been forgotten but is also the cause of wounds that have never healed, ulcers that bleed when scratched a century and a half later. You still find perfectly integrated, successful educated people with heritable lines to the original conflict arguing vehemently about it, with rancor intact as if the issues were current, and unwilling to yield to the other, analogous to a tribal conflict between competing clans in the Amazon basin. A rational argument without a discolored edge of enmity seems impossible.

It's hard to see how the stain of slavery, the original sin of modern democracy, can be dealt with unless there is an official apology, and this would belong to all the Americans. They were all complicit in it, they all agreed to it legally, and they all participated in the trade in human flesh. Therefore we should all apologize for it without thinking that this is all there is to it. It is only a starting point and the whole redress agreement will encompass all Americans, particularly the descendants of the people wronged.

There will never be any perfection in it. The stain will not be bleached out. It will still be there, but this does not mean nothing can be done about it. An apology would be a start, and only a start, but one has to start somewhere. Not starting is the default failure position.

The Real Forgotten American

When the Puritans arrived on the shores of modern day Massachusetts, there were perhaps thirty million people already living in the space of land now occupied by the United States. Today there are no more three million of their direct descendants.

The ways in which they were killed, made sick, driven off their lands, discriminated against, and held down are fairly well known. Recounting the whole sorry story cannot be done in the space of a page, as it would be condensed so much it would barely make sense. No matter what you call it, it was genocide, to the eternal shame of the globe's first enduring representative government. The loss of legacy is incalculable, and the treatment of many of the remaining native tribes is inexcusable. It is an indelible stain on American history.

You want to know who the forgotten American is? This is the forgotten American, the thousand tribes, not some miners, mechanics, mill hands, and dirt farmers who were phased out by the relentless march of economic change. Languages and legacies are completely forgotten although the descendants still remain. In the territory encompassed by the State of Oregon, dozens of distinct tribes lived, some of them speaking languages that were unique in the absolute sense of the word, unlike any other, with no known linguistic relatives. The native Americans were so far from homogeneous that it is hard to fathom. This is possibly one of the unreflective reasons why they were wiped out, because homogeneity and conformity were both highly valued by the European cultures that wiped them out.

We of the British persuasion are fond of denigrating the Spaniards and their mode of colonialism, particularly the Mexicans, but they, along with the Peruvians, Bolivians, and Paraguayans, have done more to preserve the native cultures than any American ever even considered. They did their damage early on, wiping the Aztecs and the Tlaxcaltecs off the map and so on, but in the mountains of the north and the south, the many tribes were more or less let alone, and in the Yucatán until recently, Spanish was the second language for the majority.

It is not that native tribes should be preserved as museum relics for ethnic study and theatricalized traditions for the tourist trade. Everybody can be modernized and assimilated into modern methods and practices, but their cultural legacies do not have to be destroyed in the process. You do not have to be European to drive a car, use a computer, or play an electric guitar. This is where all the native Americans have been betrayed, and their value forgotten.

WHEN SANITY BELABORS GRACE

Which border is it at when sanity
Belabors grace and turns the fall to art?
The gate is open, is it is it not?
The mysteries crawl under the fences,
They have no shame. They have no use for it,
The glitter. Stars do shine and light does walk
On shadow. Plain as day, no day is plain,
No plain is walked upon unless the trail
The walking means the gods have not been paid
Their dues, the virile gods that keep the grain
In mind. The cows don't care. Their gods are still
Until the cud comes up and must be chewed.
The antelope hide fast and disappear.
They reappear. They travel through the dirt.
Their gods walk where space is solid black.

CITY ON A HILL

So high up there it looked improbable
To get. I thought about it long and hard
Before I made my mind up. Once again
The chill, a step by step the wind in front
And peril chasing, doom the nightmare down
The mountain. Stupid men in charge and rules
That make no sense, designed they are to make
Of fools the leader's trade, whose expertise
Demands unlearnéd babbling, raging cant
Dressed up in confidence and shouted loud.
Applause rides in the breeze, the blood-scream wails
And echoes on the cliffs. The children laugh
Because it is exciting, all the flags
And pennants going ragged flapping.
Escape is not the game, there's no relief
In getting out, the grade too steep to rest
Along the slide and threaten rolling down
Halfway. The idiots will muddle on.
Up there it stands. No stopping now. Press on.

STIR YOUR SOUP

The smell of failure boiling permeates
The mind. It breaks the magic down, oh yes
The magic in the tragedy evolved,
The poetry of love, the scent of sex
When life was good and time was madness spent
In ecstasy before the crash, the burn,
Recovery in bandages, the spell
Of memory, amnesiac, the lies
You told yourself, the spices ground by hand,
The custom flavors pulverized so fine,
The potpourri of heartache, magic sauce
Of misery transformed. When you feel
The world has changed enough to make you well,
The time has come for you to stir your soup.

THE SOUND OF LAUGHTER

A wild and rangy sky, the wind-complaint
A bitter moan addressing windows shut
Up tighter than a loan shark's lips the time
You need a break. Trees wave too hard to keep
Their branches on, the clouds drawn by the mad,
The chainsaw killers in the heavens rent
By seeping blood on tattered edges. No,
An orange wash betrays the wind, the clouds
Too pretty for the ranting raving gale.
A bright sky rises up and all the dark
Gray demons disappear into the light.
The crazy wind blows on like nothing wrong
Into the day as bright as babies' eyes
When mother reaches down to pick them up.
The wind drives leaves up off the ground and sends
Them flying down the street. Around the world
The sound of laughter drowns the furies out.

<u>Who</u> <u>Are</u> <u>These</u> <u>Americans?</u>

There is one thing about the American polity that has never changed. This is the querulous, unsteady relationship between liberty and equality that has plagued the American republic from the very beginning. A shifting narrowness of view has persisted throughout all the forms that characterize the cultural evolution. Freedom of manners, the willingness to accept minor differences in favor of general agreement, is not a staple value of American culture. From early 19th century hill-folk alarmism in far northwest Appalachia that the Kingdom of God was coming for them and them only, to the deluded pietism of current Florida Congressman Francis Rooney that the FBI is a haven for secret agents of the Deep State, liberty of belief has challenged equality of law and circumstance .

This dissonance was present in the Founding Fathers, who waged a long war to get the vote. When they won it, they restricted it to property-owners, themselves in other words. It is represented in the political sentiments of Green candidate Jill Stein, whose natural allies should be liberal Democrats but whose sympathies have found a friend in the autocrat Vladimir Putin, and by extension the proto-fascists of the alt-right. It is a disunity familiar in American history, epitomized by the Church of Latter Day Saints searching for freedom by wanting to found an independent republic in the American frontier. Non-Mormons there would be discriminated against by religious law, if not banned and exiled.

In the vast rangelands of the central prairies, the Southwest, and the Great Basin highlands, the cattle barons set up shop in unfenced territory to let the cattle forage at will. Reluctantly, they allowed competing ranchers to use the water and range rights. They could hardly do more, open range being basically indefensible. They did not feel the same way about sheep herders. They justified their disdain for sheep on pasture destruction, but in truth it was a cultural value. The cattle ranchers did not routinely shoot cattle other than their own but they did routinely shoot sheep. Equality of treatment did not extend to the sheep handlers. Real American men did not run sheep. Outcasts like the Irish and the Basque did.

The idea that liberty's default use is to harm the equality of others runs through American history like a system of interconnected highways. This is what happens when corporate entities remunerate politicians to suppress the vote, and when succeeding generations find fault, but not success, in the parents who raised them to have good judgment. Liberty is a beauty contest sponsored by people fond of their own ambition, and mutual dependency is the consolation prize for also-rans. Equality is a leveling exercise designed to populate the bottom of the heap.

SLOBDOPE AND THE HAIRLESS: a Neolithic fairy tale

They were running and running. Then they ran some more. Their chests felt like they were breathing rocks, their throats were sore, and their legs seemed like they would seize up and fall off.

Then the screaming started. Blood was everywhere.

The screaming would not stop. Slobdope sat bolt upright from the skins and straw he slept on and found himself screaming at the top of his lungs. Wonderflower was shaking him and staring with big eyes. Little Shrimpscatter's face was twisted up with terror. Even Sneeth raised up on one elbow and studied Slobdope with his one good eye. The dent on the side of Sneeth's head was clearly visible in the flickering light of the campfire casting a red glow on the interior. After a few moments Slobdope stopped screaming and looked around like he had no idea where he was. He did have no idea where he was, and he was befuddled, confused, and mystified. Wonderflower stroked him on the arm. Then she put her hand between his legs, and Slobdope's boneless limb started growing a bone inside it. Slobdope was beginning to realize where he was. Wonderflower bent down between his legs and took his bone in her mouth. Now Slobdope knew where he was. After a minute, when the knob on the end of his bone swelled up and its one eye poked out from the skin, Wonderflower rolled over on her back and spread her legs. Slobdope hopped on top and slipped his bone into the wonderfully warm wetness.

Little Shrimpscatter studied every move with her eyes wide and shining. Sneeth grunted and rolled his one good eye and laid back down to sleep.

Slobdope definitely knew where he was now.

That morning Sneeth and Slobdope sat on a couple of big rocks in front of the hut and watched Wonderflower and Shrimpscatter down by the water with most of their clothing off. Slobdope knocked a chip off the spear point he was crafting and looked at Sneeth looking at the girls. "Aren't they fantastic, Sneeth?" Slobdope said. "Look at that. No hair on their bodies except for a little on the arms and legs...And you know where. And those big butts!"

"Ooo-woo, woo woo woo! Bow wow wow!" said Sneeth.

"You said it." Slobdope's boneless limb rose up and bounced a little. He put the spear point down and walked to the girls. Wonderflower looked at him and looked at his crotch and shook her head. "No way," she said. "You smell like a dead deer." She went back to the pieces of tree bark the girls had been soaking and tearing into strips.

"Please?" Slobdope begged.

"No way. You stink!"

Slobdope looked over at Shrimpscatter. She was looking him dead in the eye. Before he had a clue what was coming, Wonderflower smacked his face with a big strip of wet bark so hard it knocked him off balance. "Don't you dare look at Shrimpscatter like that." And she smacked him again.

"What?" Slobdope said. He rubbed his face where the skin was a hot red. "What did you do that for?"

"I told you."

Slobdope looked at Shrimpscatter with a lost expression and she looked back wistfully and then saw her older sister glaring at her with fire in her eyes. Shrimp hurried up with the bark-peeling and looked down at the dirt.

Slobdope just stood there.

"What do you want now?" Wonderflower demanded to know.

Sneeth shuffled up, dragging his bad leg. "Do we have anything to eat later?" Slobdope asked.

"Grubs and mashed acorns." Sneeth shuffled back where he was.

"We had grubs and mashed acorns yesterday. I'm sick of grubs and mashed acorns," Slobdope whined.

"Go get us some meat then," Wonderflower said angrily.

"You know how much work it is to run down rabbits?"

Sneeth chimed into the conversation. "Reeble rabble rabble tick dork go do wham bam boom!" he said.

Slobdope looked at him. "Be quiet, Sneeth."

"He's telling you something," Wonderflower said.

"He's babbling away like usual."

Wonderflower stood up shaking so hard with anger her breasts were bobbling up and down. "Slobdope, you are so...so...How to put it? Your mind is like a walnut." Before he could fathom how wonderful it was to be compared to a walnut, that little kernel of precious meat trapped in that hard shell, he caught sight of the hard look Wonderflower was fixing on him. "Sneeth is telling you something," she said. "He is telling you to build a deadfall trap."

"A what?"

She explained to Slobdope how it worked. The blank look on his face told her that his wonderful walnut was incapable of comprehending a deadfall trap. "Oh go on and do what you do," she said in disgust.

"At least I don't think that Sneeth makes sense," Slobdope said. "If he does, you should've heard what he just said about you."

She picked up the strip of bark, and he hurried off.

They ran, they ran, they ran and they ran. They ran until their legs gave out, and they heard The Killers crashing through the brush behind them, and they gathered themselves together and ran some more. The screaming started up, and the blood was everywhere and the screaming turned into a loud gurgling and then the big rock. Slobdope sat upright in a cold sweat. He saw the big shape looming over him and the screaming started up again.

It was him screaming, only he was awake. Wonderflower was awake and staring at the big shape blocking the firelight. Shrimpscatter was awake and trembling violently in terror. Sneeth was awake and his one good eye was trained on the big shape. He knew who it was. He only wondered how Habubblegojiggum could be here. He was dead.

"Shut up, Slobdope," Habubblegojiggum shouted. "Shut your rotten mouth." He picked Slobdope off the ground and held him upright. Slobdope stopped screaming.

"You're alive, Habubble."

"No, I'm only pretending."

"No, you're alive."

"Good grief, you're stupid."

"How did you get here?"

"I flew like a bird."

"You did?"

Habubblegojiggum dropped Slobdope back on his pallet. "No thanks to you." He turned to put his face toward the light and ripped his garments away from his throat, to reveal the angry red scar on his neck. "You didn't cut me deep enough, though."

"You wouldn't shut up, Habubblegojiggum. The Killers were catching up. I saved your life."

"You wanted to kill me."

"I wanted you to shut up. That's why I had to pick up the rock. You wouldn't shut up, even with your throat cut."

Habubblegojiggum picked Slobdope up again and shook him by the shoulders. "You tried to kill me, you idiot. You cut my throat."

"The Killers would've could killed you for sure if I hadn't knocked you out. You're the idiot. You didn't get the message when I cut you. That's why I hit you with the rock."

Habubblegojiggum dropped him again. "There's no talking to you. How did I get mixed up with such an idiot?"

Now Slobdope stood up on his own and shoved Habubblegojiggum hard in the chest. The big man backed up a step. "How? How?" Slobdope asked. "You're too good to do any work, too scared to fight, too slow to run...and you won't shut up. That's all you can do. Talk."

"Got anything to eat?"

"That's the other thing you can do. Eat."

It was early in the morning, and the sky was turning from black to blue in the east. Slobdope, Habubblegojiggum, Sneeth, and Shrimpscatter sat on the big rocks outside the hut while

Wonderflower mashed the acorns and spitted the grubs on green sticks to broil them over the cooking fire.

"Grubs and mashed acorns?" Habubblegojiggum asked.

"That's what we got," Slobdope affirmed, curling his lip in revulsion.

"What is this that?" Habubblegojiggum asked, turning and looking the hut over. "It looks like a roof. Why did you build it like that?"

Slobdope looked astonished. "Well, of course it's a roof."

"Where's the rest of it?"

Through fits and starts, after much hesitating, beating around the bush, and waffling back and forth, Slobdope explained that the top part of the structure had to be built first. Otherwise there would be no way to put the roof on top of the walls. Besides, if they had built the walls first, there would be nothing to hold them in place while the top was put on."

Now it was Habubblegojiggum's turn to be astonished. Listening with his mouth dropped open, finally he blurted out, "How did you think you would get the walls under the roof?"

"Little by little."

"You're an idiot."

"So that's when it happened to Sneeth."

"You mean the dent in his head."

"Yup."

"The first pile of rocks came crashing down."

"Up doop ding ding faw daw wham bam boom," Sneeth said, studying the two of them with his one good eye.

Habubblegojiggum looked at Slobdope. "You're not only an idiot. You are dangerous."

The food was ready. The girls finished first, and went down to the water to resume their tree bark business. They shucked off most of their clothing, and that got Habubblegojiggum's attention. His eyes dilated and his lips quivered. "How about letting me have some of that for dessert," he said, pointing at Wonderflower.

"I think you better leave," Slobdope said.

"How about that, then?" He asked, pointing to Shrimpscatter.

"She's little, Habubble."

With that, Habubblegojiggum jumped up, walked over to Shrimpscatter and ripped off the rest of her clothing. Wonderflower and Shrimpscatter froze in fear. Habubblegojiggum was a huge man. "She may be little, but she has one of these," he said as he drove a finger between her legs and inside her wet place. Shrimpscatter gasped in shock and wonder.

Wonderflower started giggling. When Habubblegojiggum whirled the little girl around and bent her over, Wonderflower was laughing hard.

Habubblegojiggum exposed his little stiff rod and put it inside Shrimpscatter and rocked back and forth until he was done. It took about ten strokes. Wonderflower was laughing so hard she could no longer stand up, and she sat down on the dirt, still laughing.

"You're the idiot," Slobdope said as Habubblegojiggum walked back and sat down on his rock.

"I may be an idiot, but I'm taking over," he said.

This stopped Wonderflower from laughing. "What did you say?"

"You've got one idiot, one babbling idiot, and you're two girls. You need someone who can think."

"Who can talk, you mean," Slobdope said.

"Hoo bee ba ba ree bop bigges idi," said Sneeth.

"I can think," said Wonderflower.

"You're a girl," Habubblegojiggum said. "You can't do anything."

"I can think," Shrimpscatter said quietly, a little bashful. "And I think you're a big bear, pushing everyone around."

Undeterred, Habubblegojiggum turned to Slobdope. "You take Wonderflower and I'll take the little one."

"Not while I'm around," said Wonderflower. "Not yet anyway."

"I'll just kill you, and Slobdope and I will share the little one."

"You kill her and I'll kill you," Slobdope said.

"Then I'll just kill you first."

Slobdope looked hard at Habubblegojiggum. "You kill me and she'll go with you. She'll go with you. She'll make you comfortable. She'll take her time. She'll do everything you want. Then one day you'll go to sleep with both eyes closed and you'll never see the morning light again."

"In that case, I'll go find The Killers, make a deal, and come back with them."

"Do do na nana aw wee kee kee kee feest," Sneeth said, fixing his one good eye on Habubblegojiggum.

"Shut up," Slobdope and Habubblegojiggum said in unison.

Wonderflower looked at them, pointed at Sneeth and said, "If you try to go now, he said, we will all kill you. Fast."

Both Slobdope and Habubblegojiggum stared speechless at Sneeth, but for different reasons. Slobdope finally realized that Sneeth did speak and that Wonderflower understood him and he knew then that Sneeth had more sense than any of them. He was in awe. He turned his eyes to Wonderflower. He cleared his throat. He turned back to Habubblegojiggum. "That's right, Habubble. We'll all kill you."

Habubblegojiggum finally realized how much trouble he was in. He tried to think fast. He was not any good at thinking, much less thinking fast. He thought of running. He was not any good at that. He thought of fighting but he was clumsy and it was three against one. Even Sneeth might help somehow. He got scared.

"That's right," Wonderflower said. "All of us."

"That's right," echoed Shrimpscatter.

"Da die!" Sneeth said emphatically.

That night when Slobdope and Wonderflower bedded down, she said, "Come over and warm me up, Slobdope." He scooted over and put his arms around her. She whispered in his ear, "You did good today."

"You told me, my mind is like a walnut. There's not much there, but it's pretty tasty."

"There's only one thing. I'll teach you how to wash. Okay?"

"Okay."

"Okay."